LAS VEGAS SHOWGIRLS

COLORING BOOK

By Rock Roulade Cocoon Collective

In Vegas, where the lights
aglow,
Showgirls dazzle, stealing
the show.
Feathers, rhinestones in
costumes rare,
Defying gravity, they dance
on air.
With poise and grace, they
all agree,
Their smiles and style, a sight
to see.
But when they dance, oh,
the funny whirls,
In the land of luck, it's Las
Vegas showgirls!

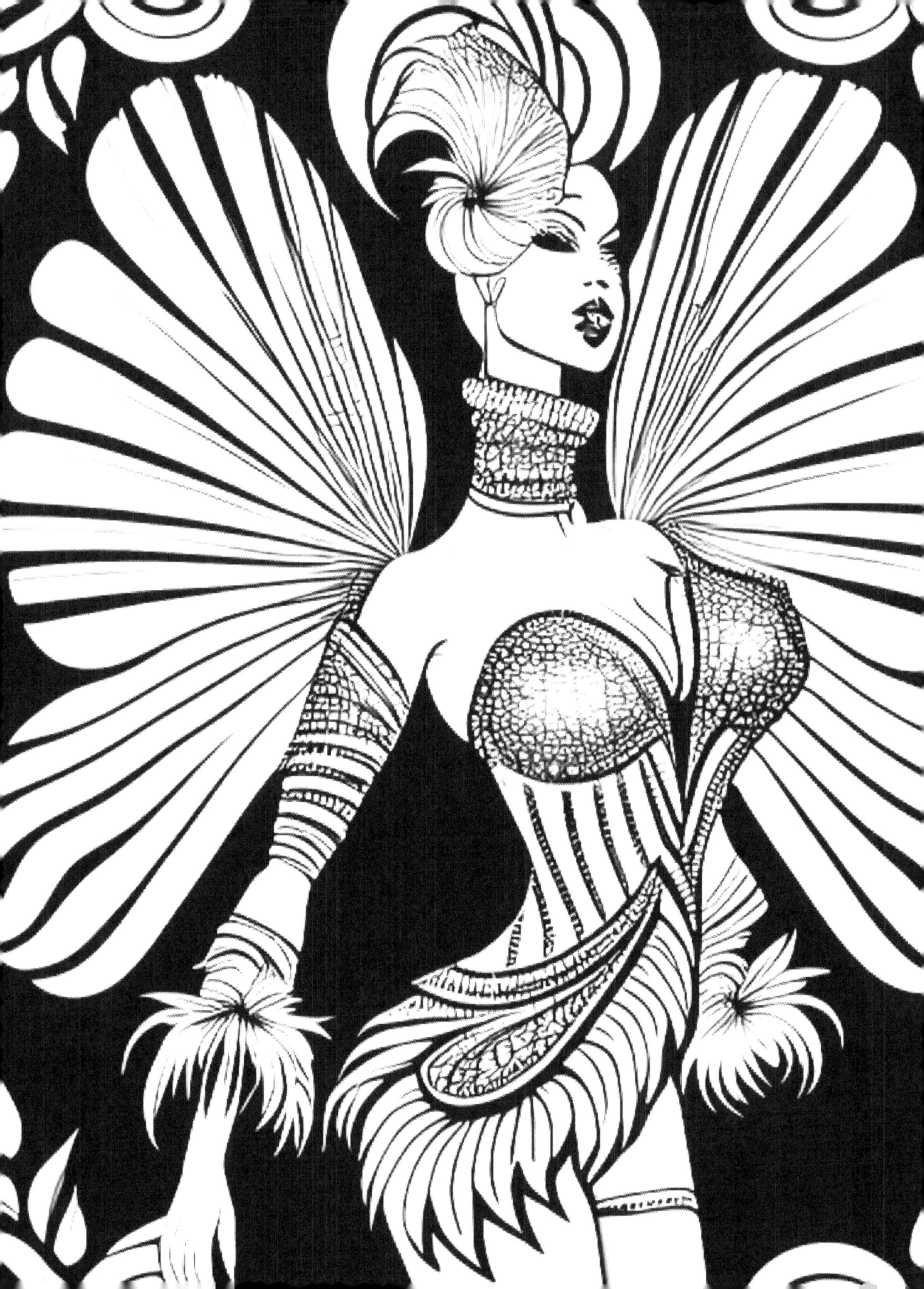

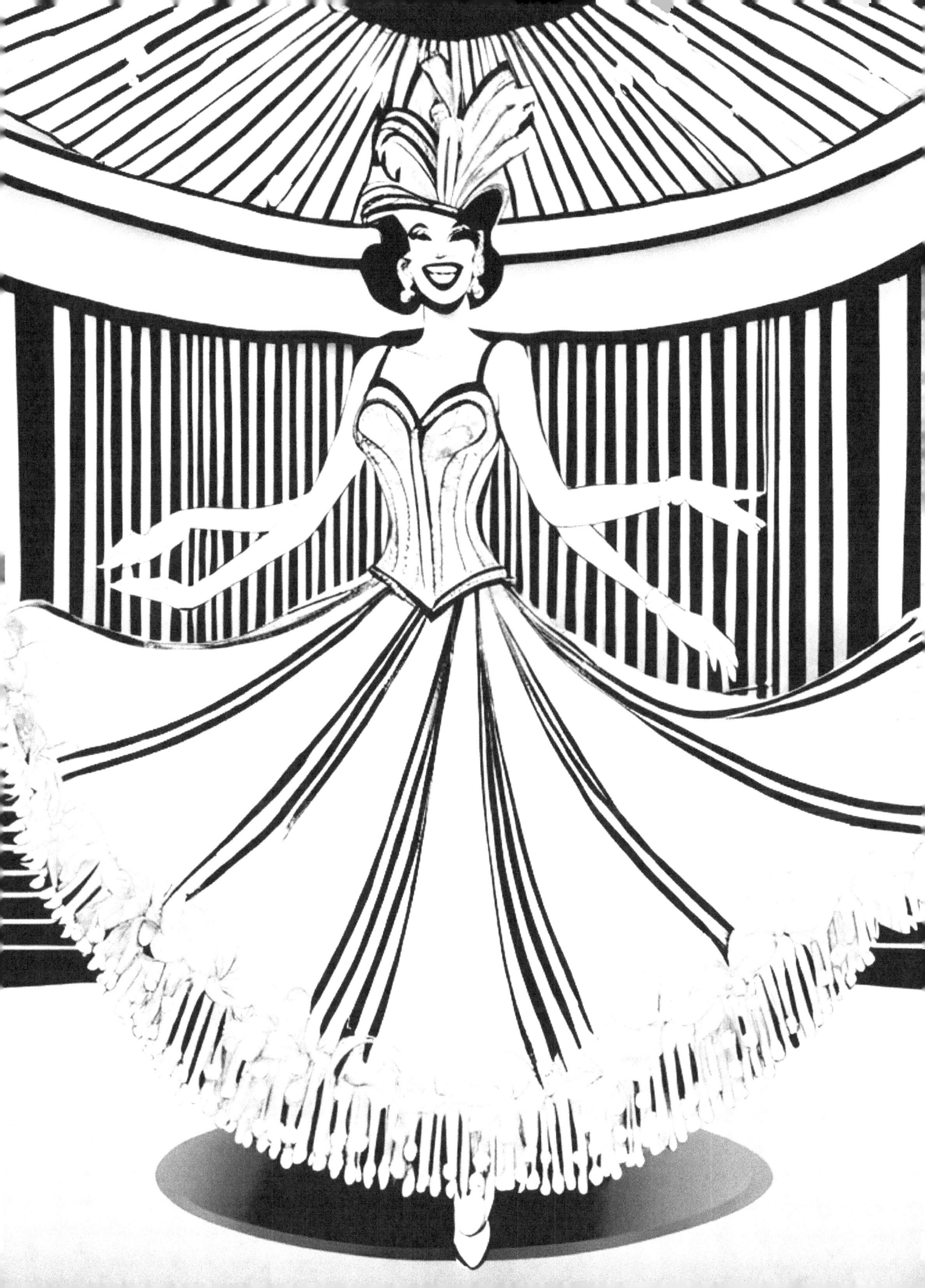

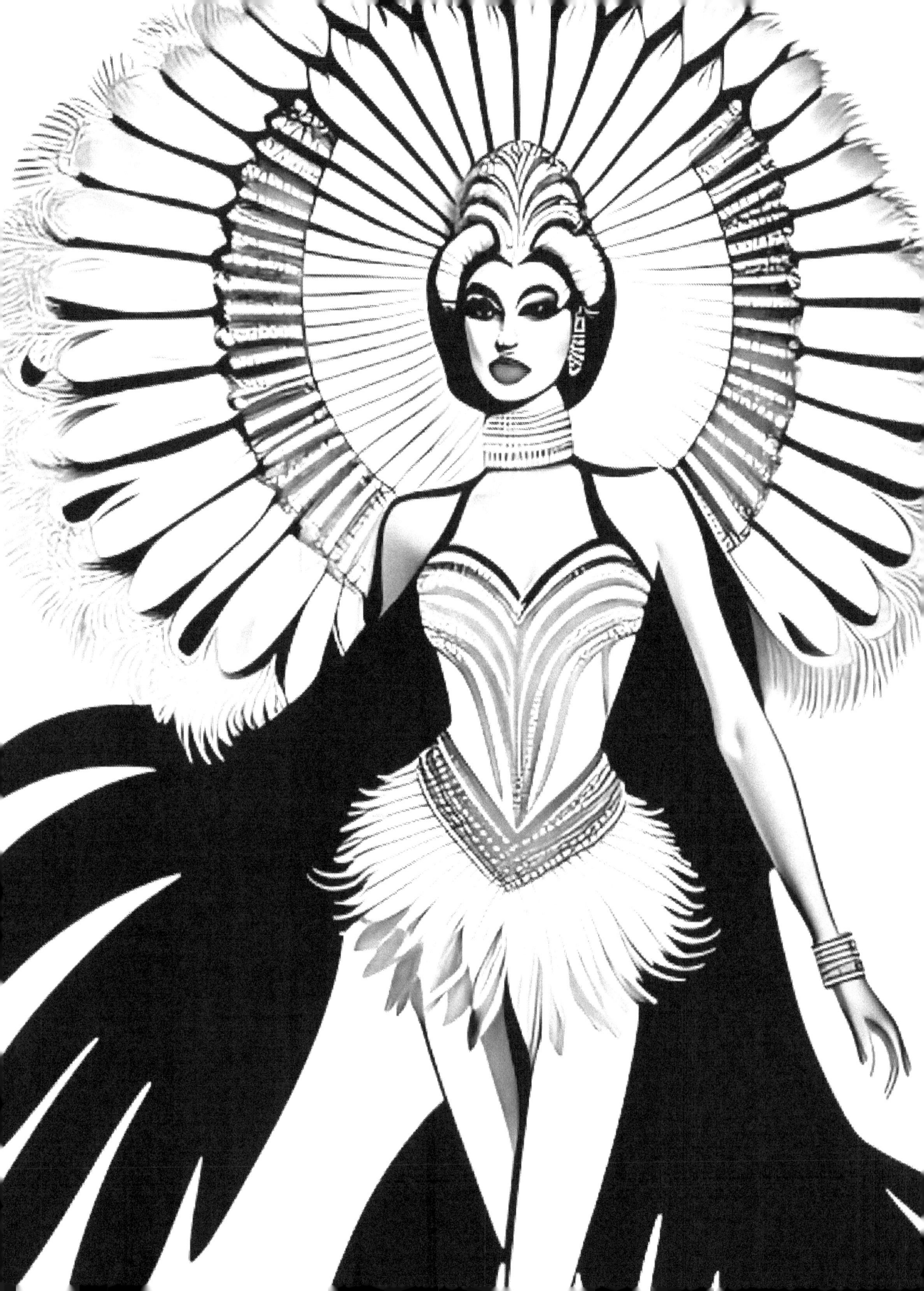

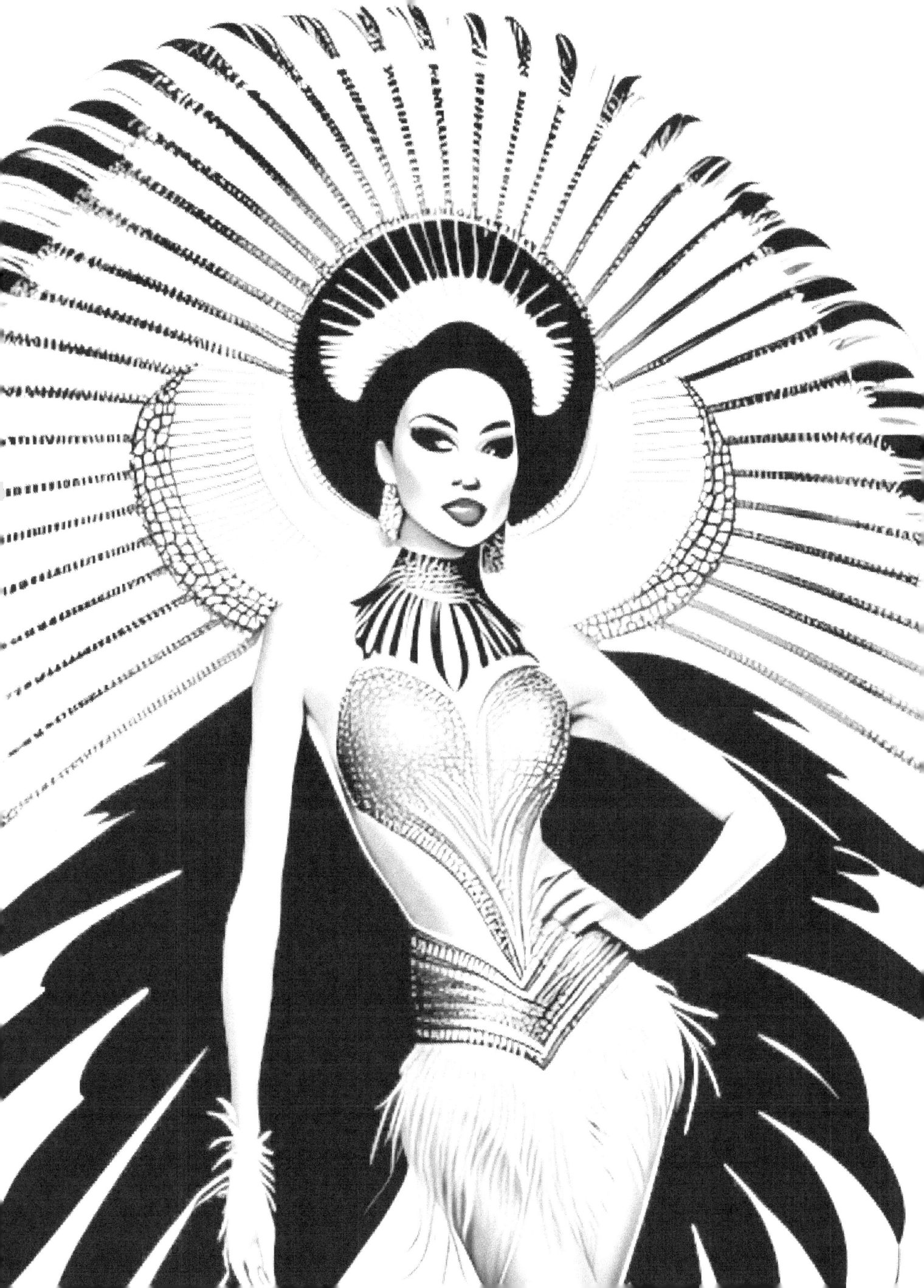

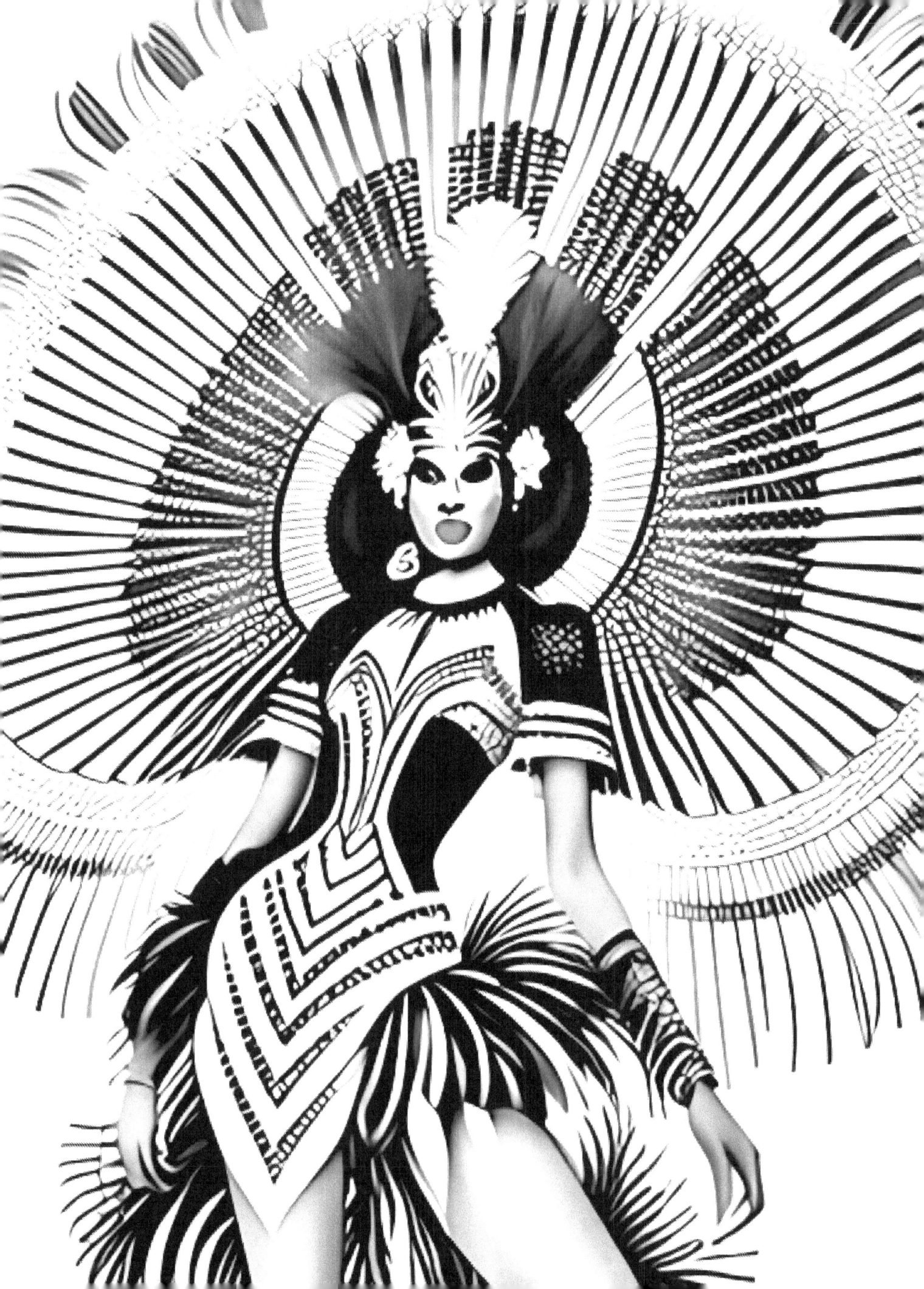

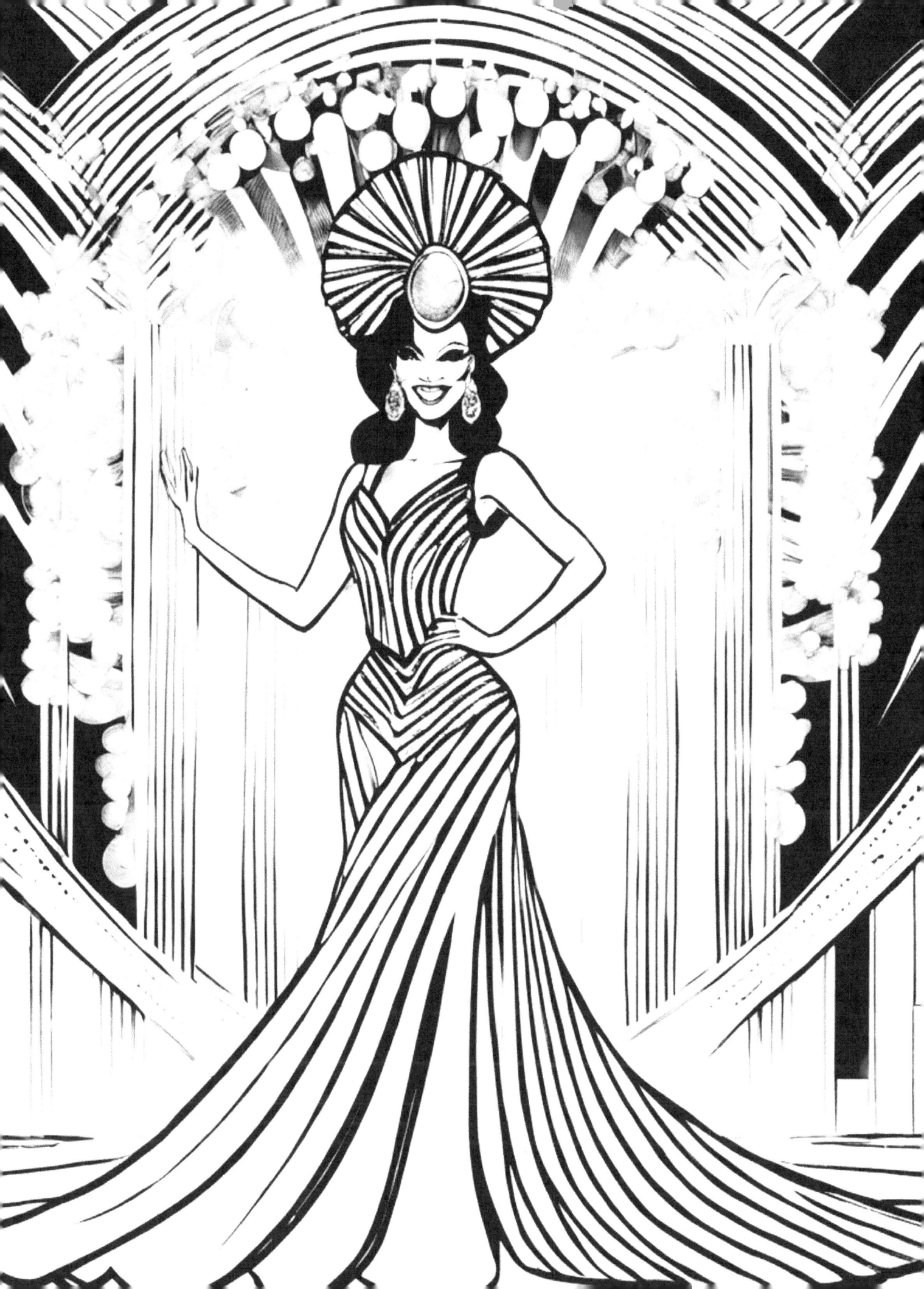

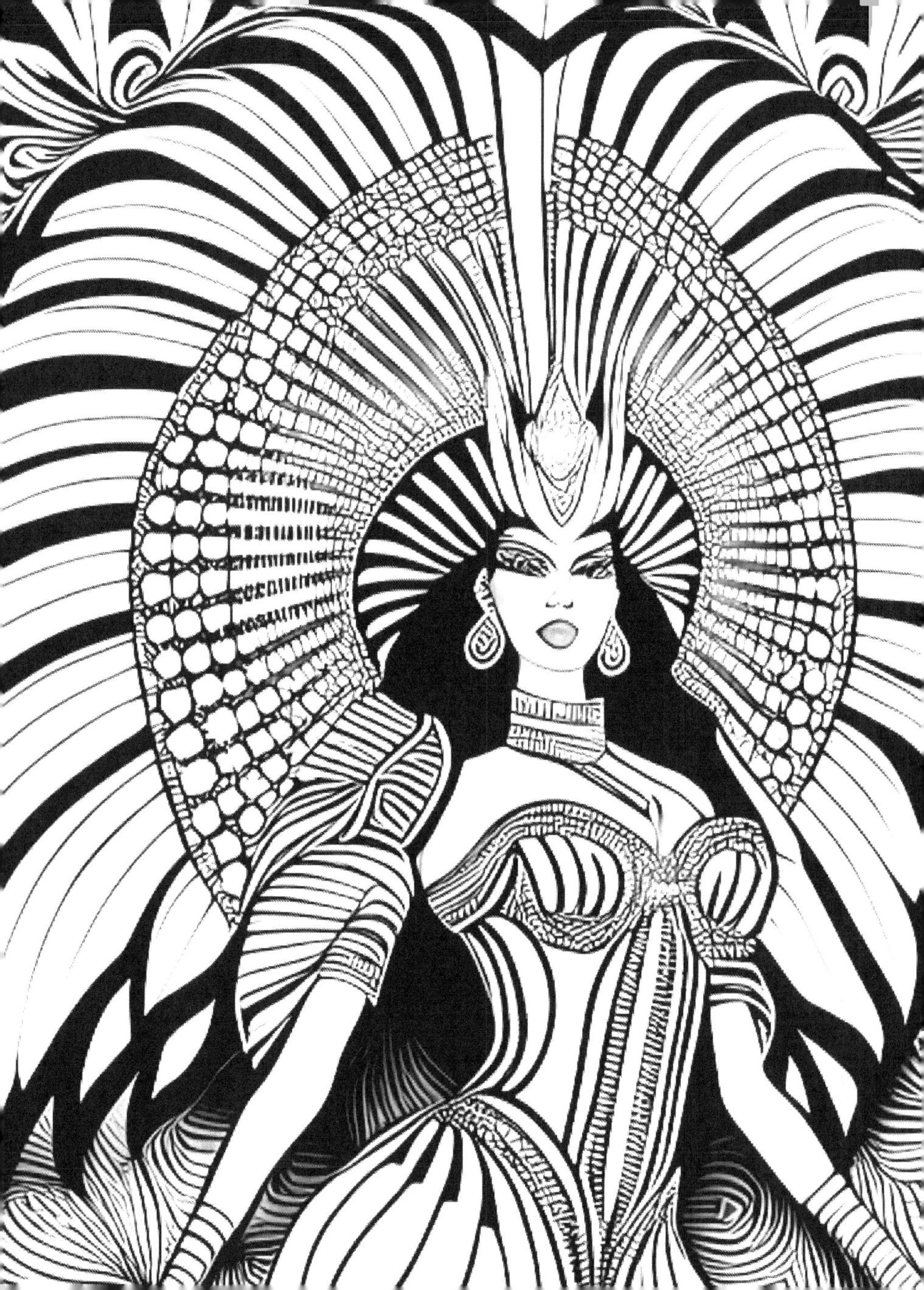

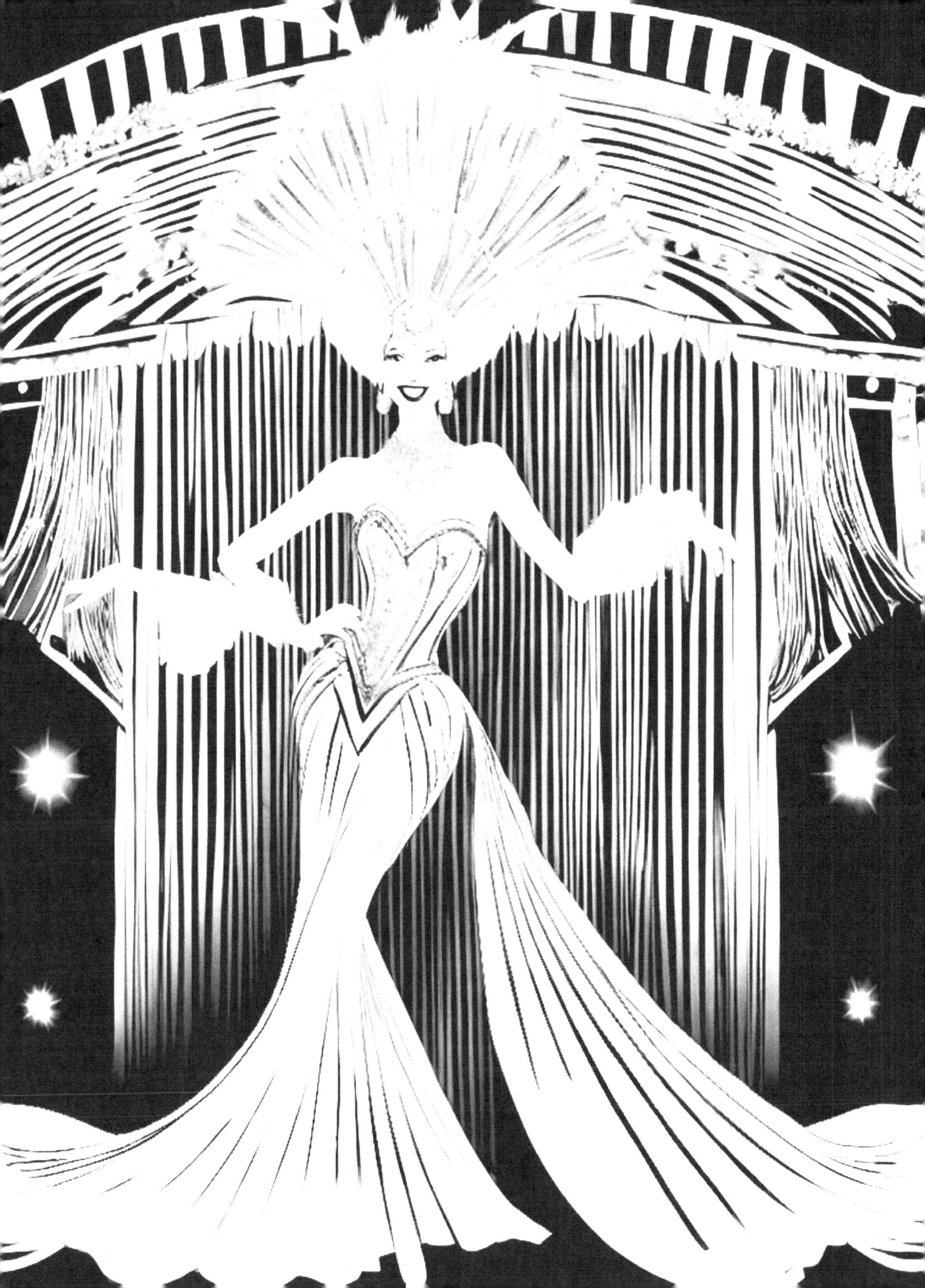

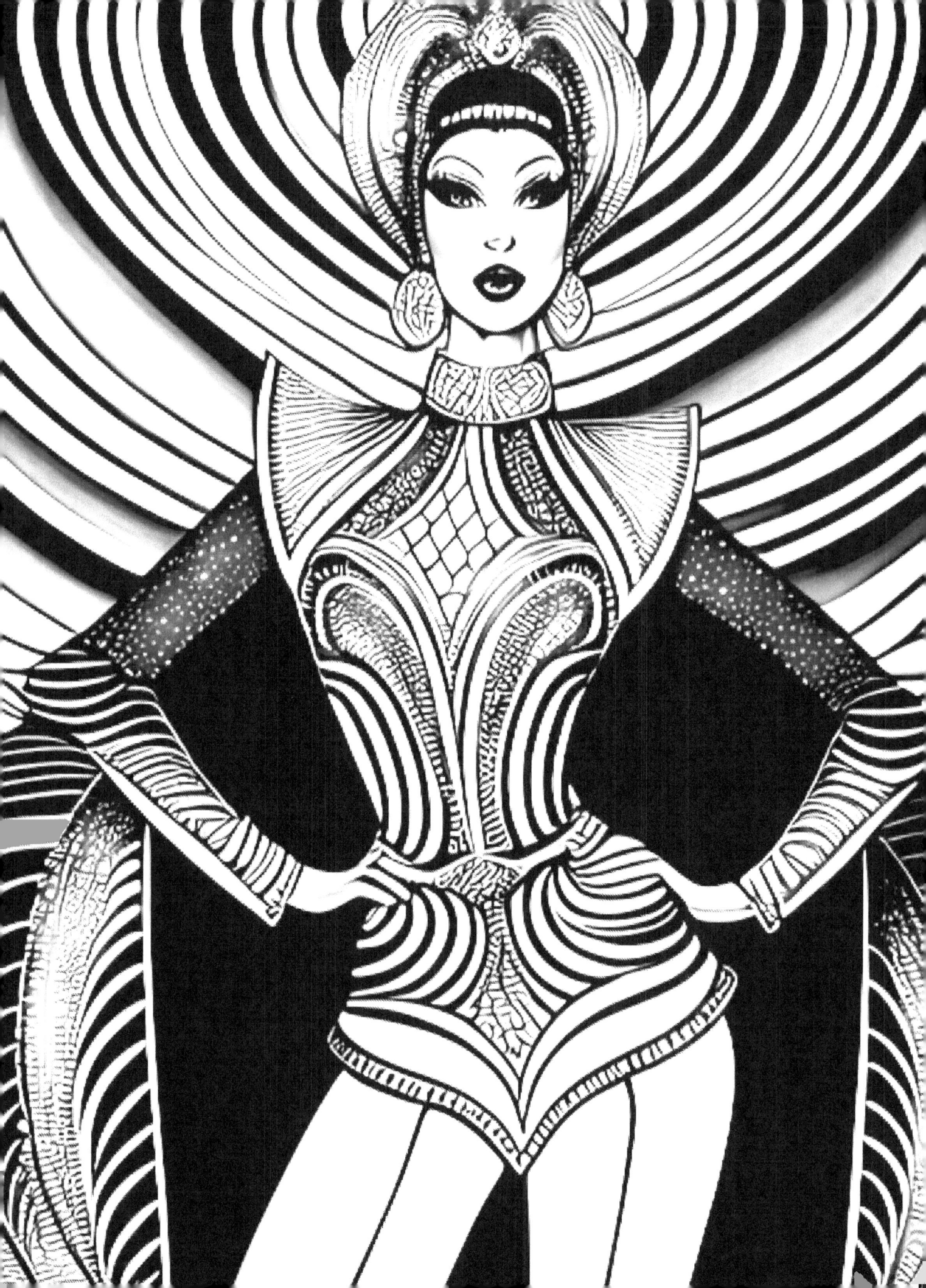

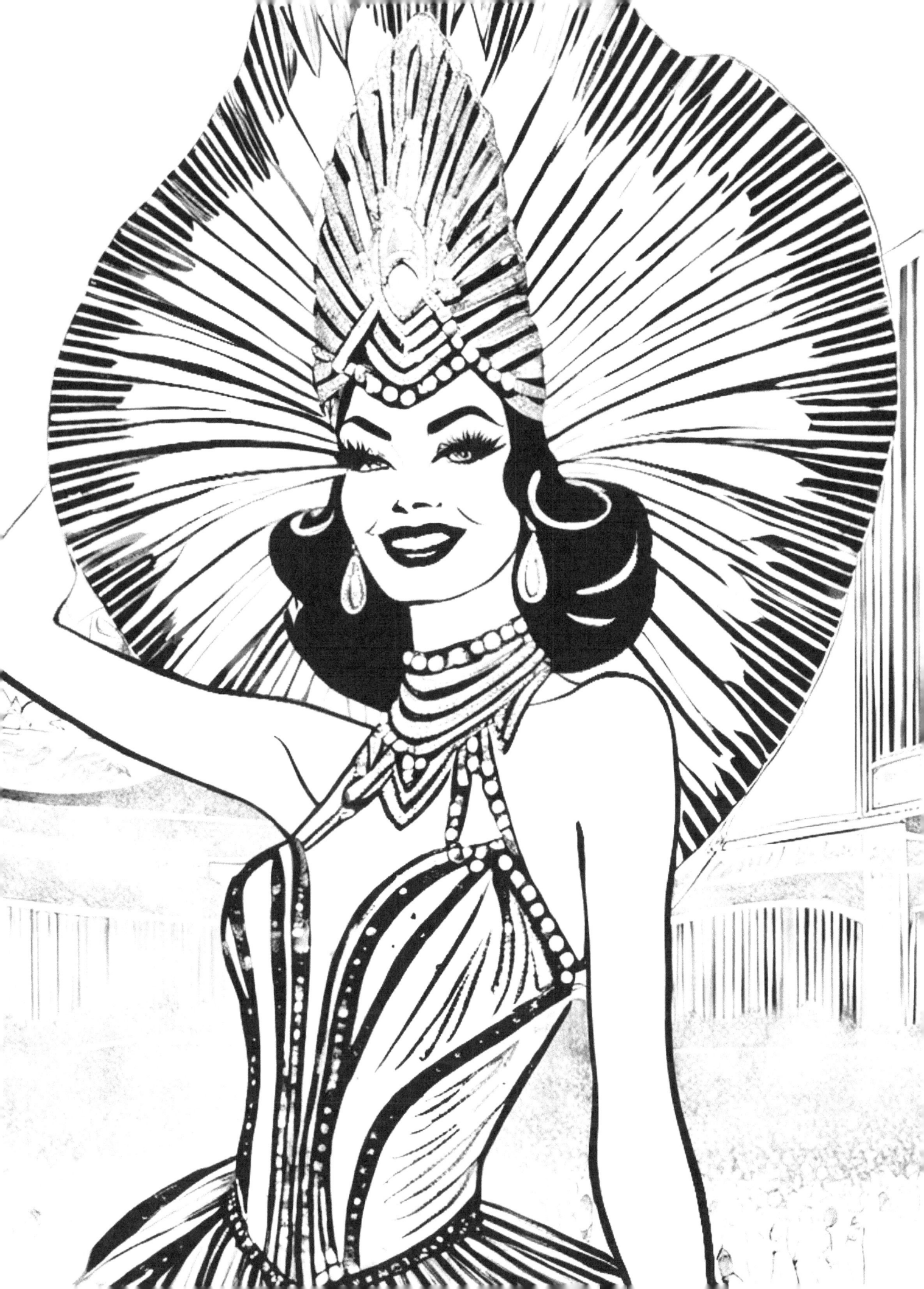

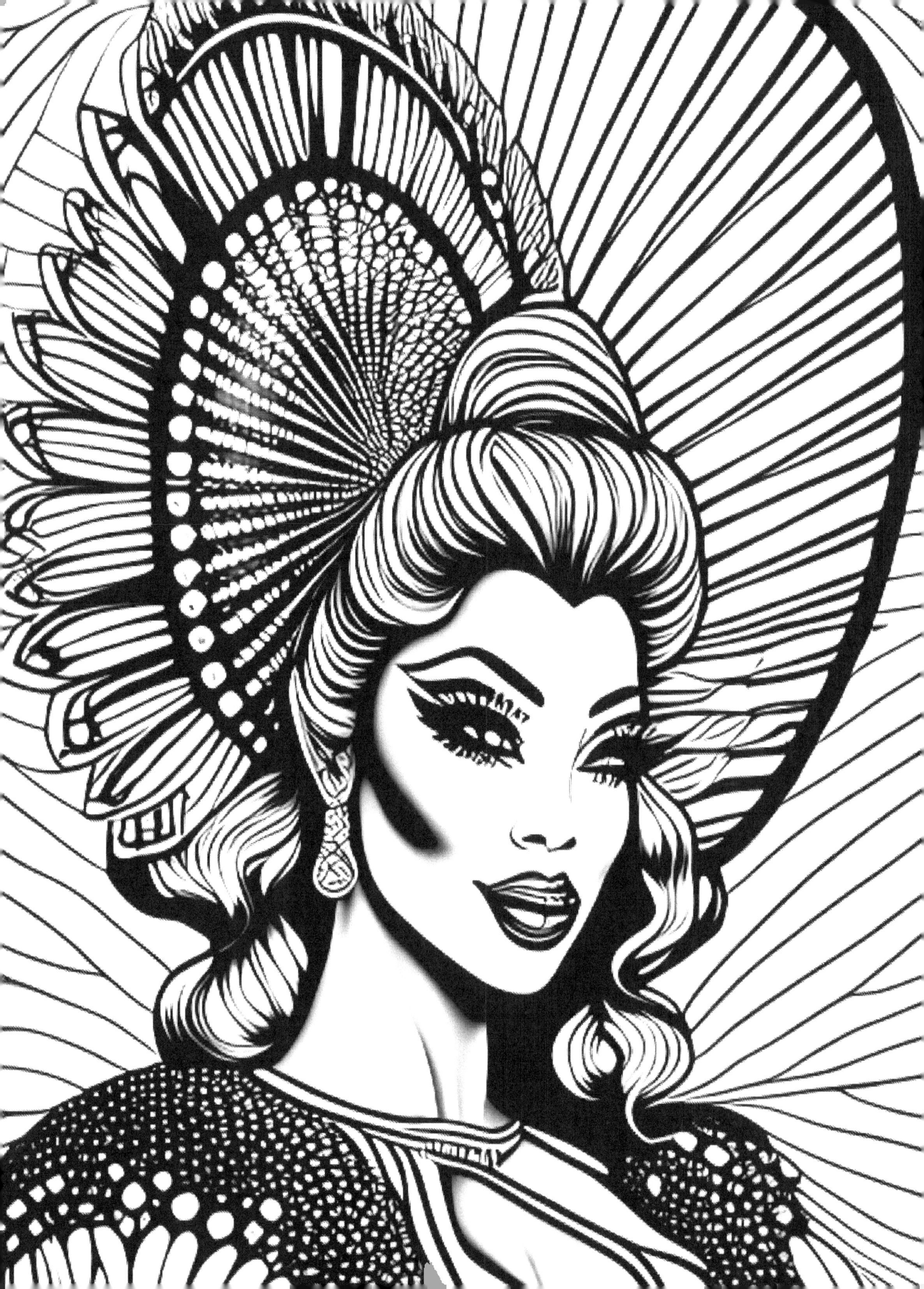

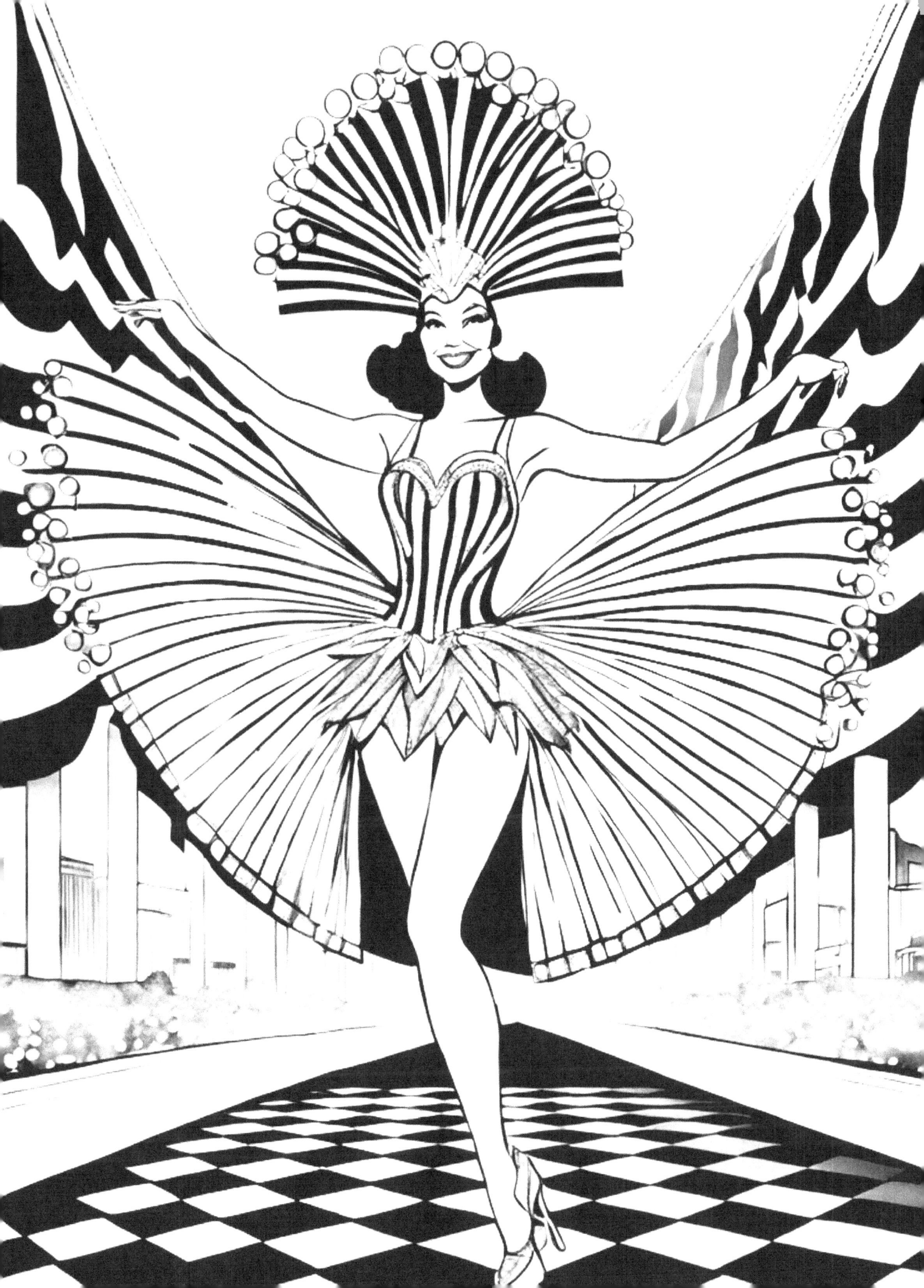

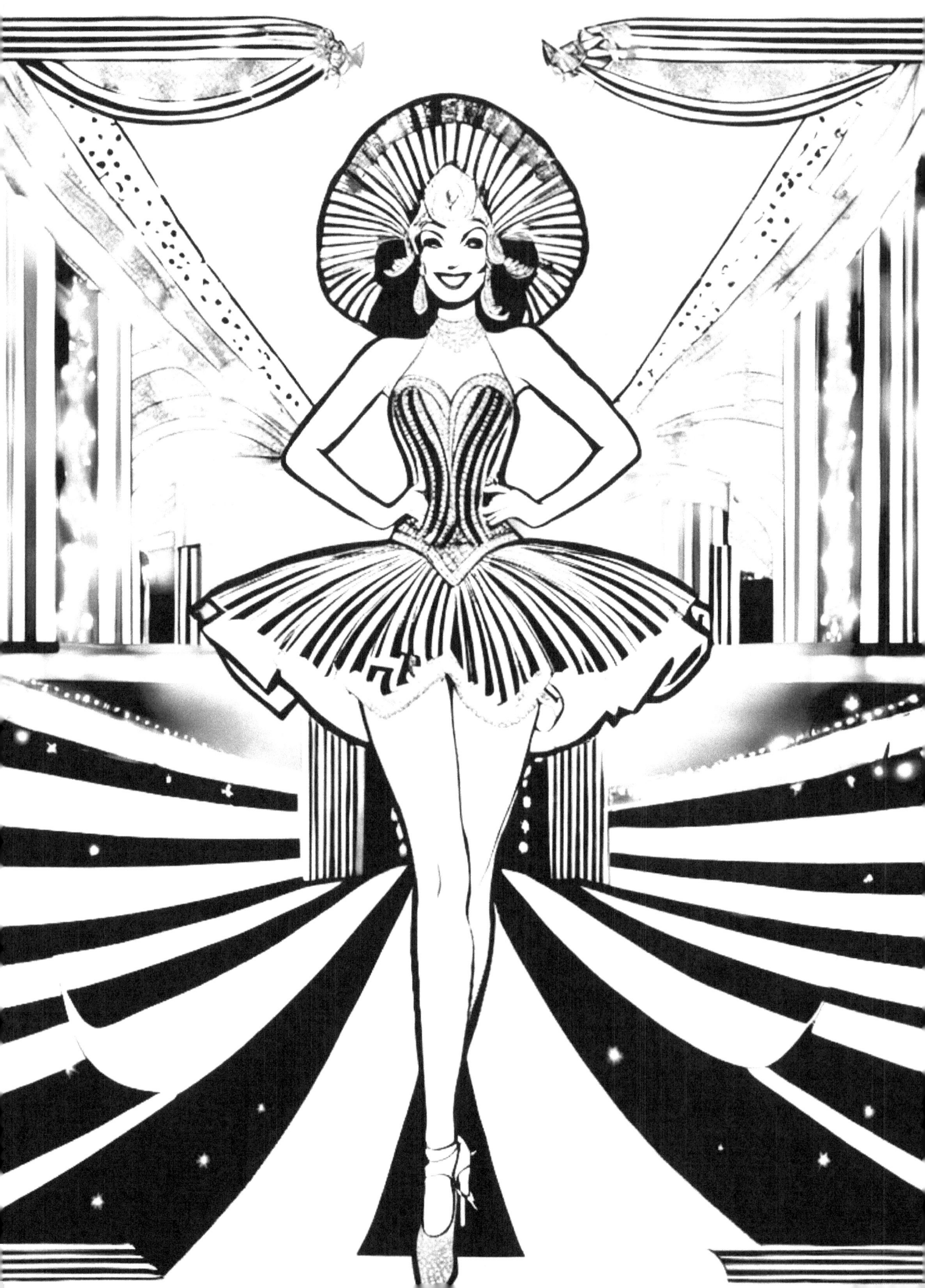

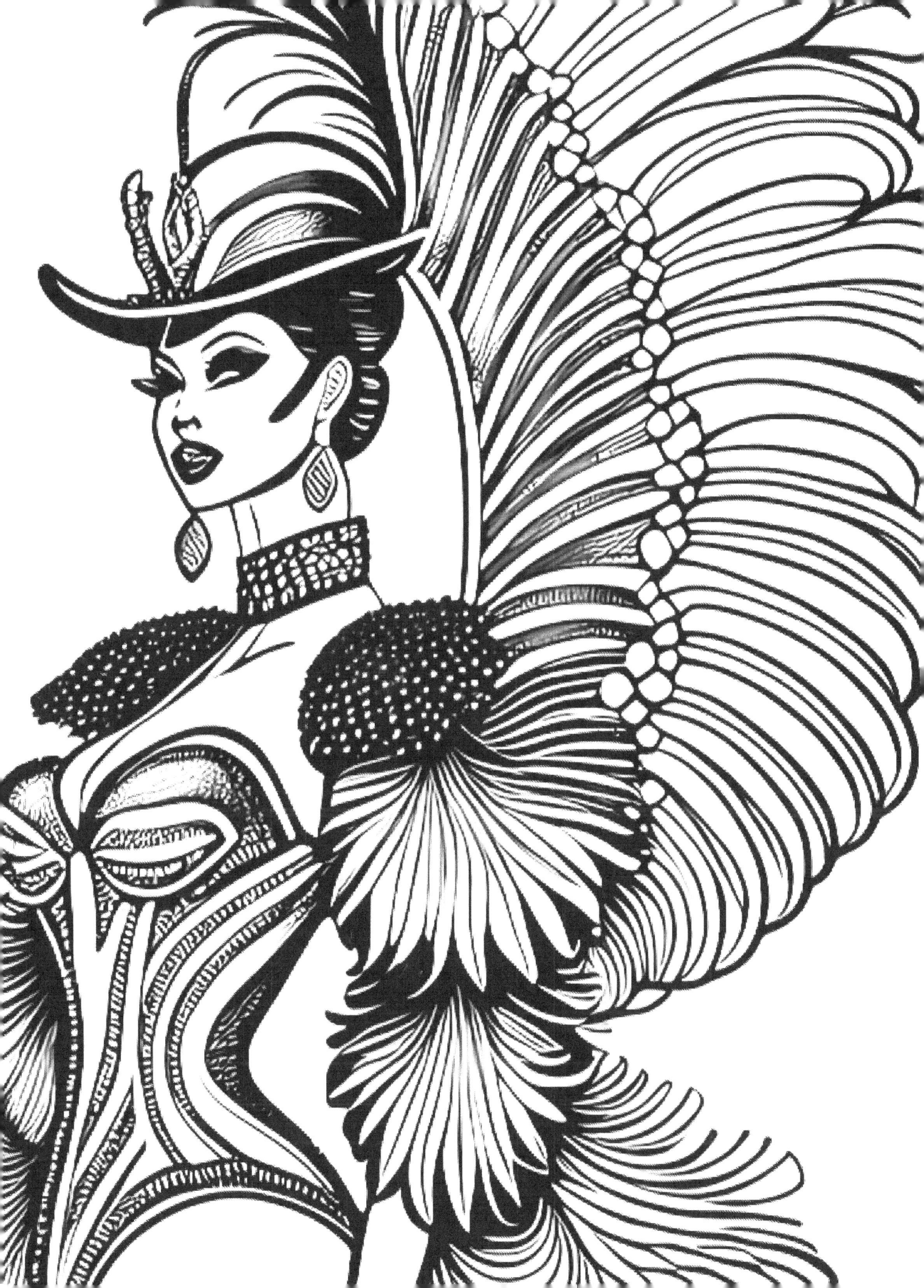

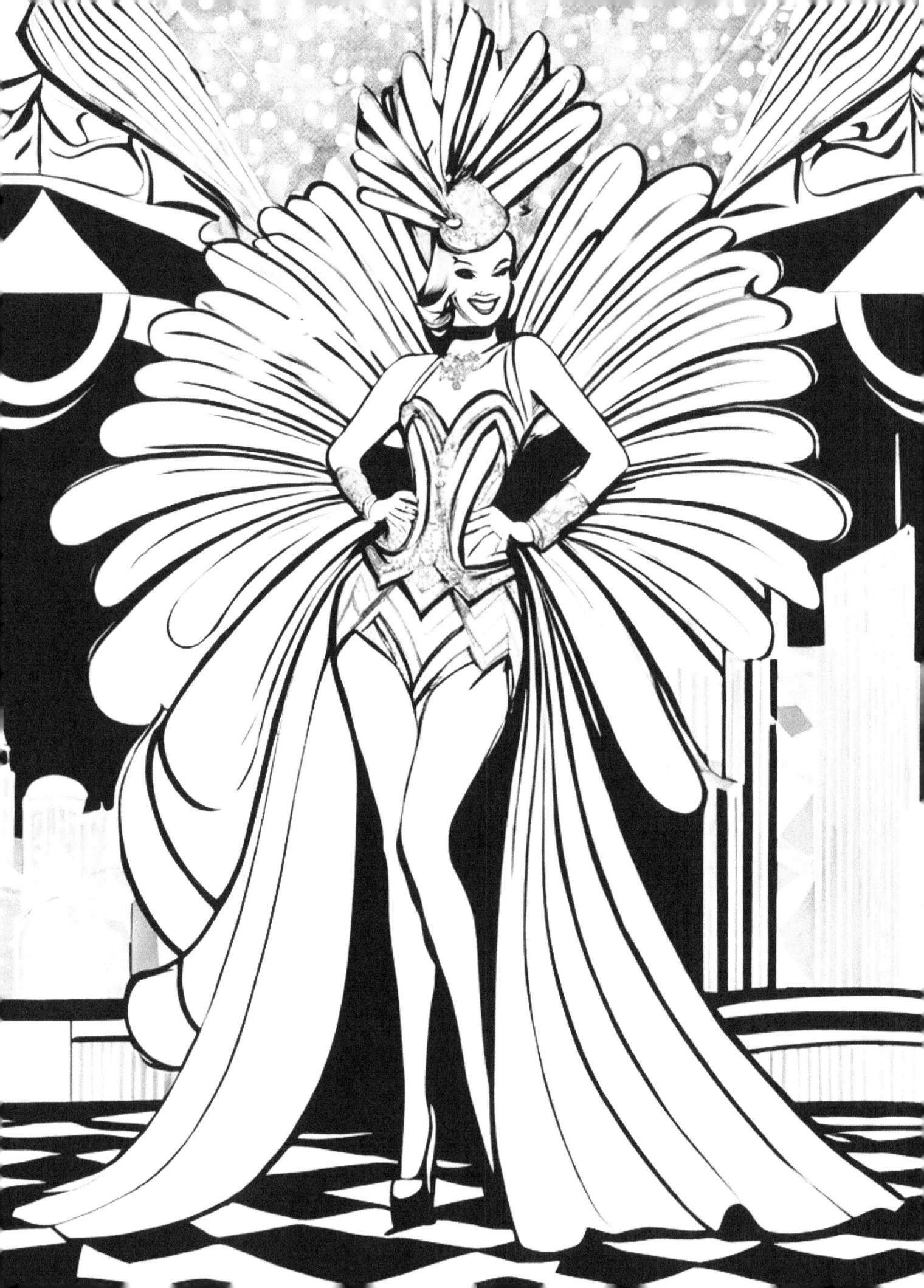

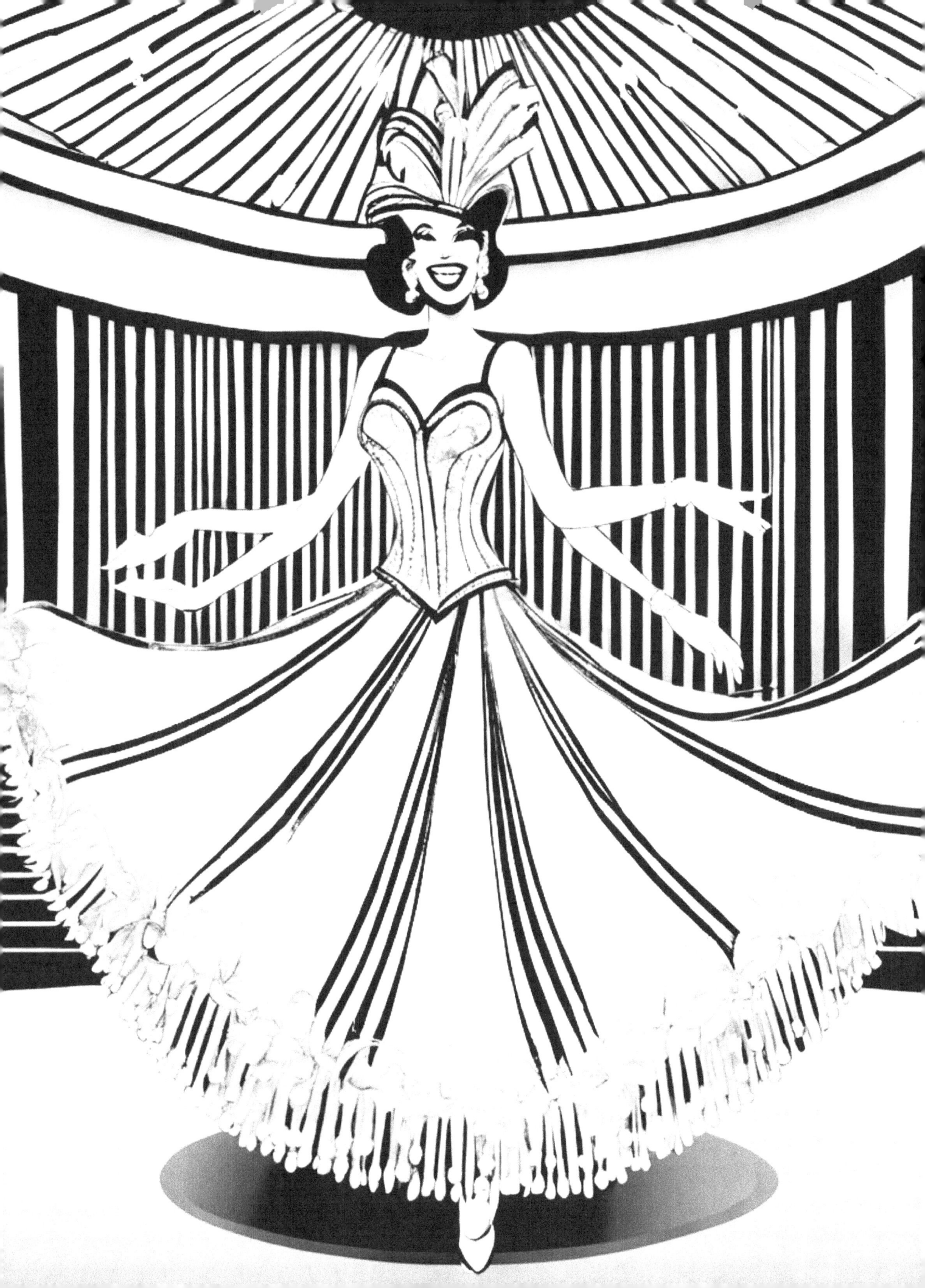

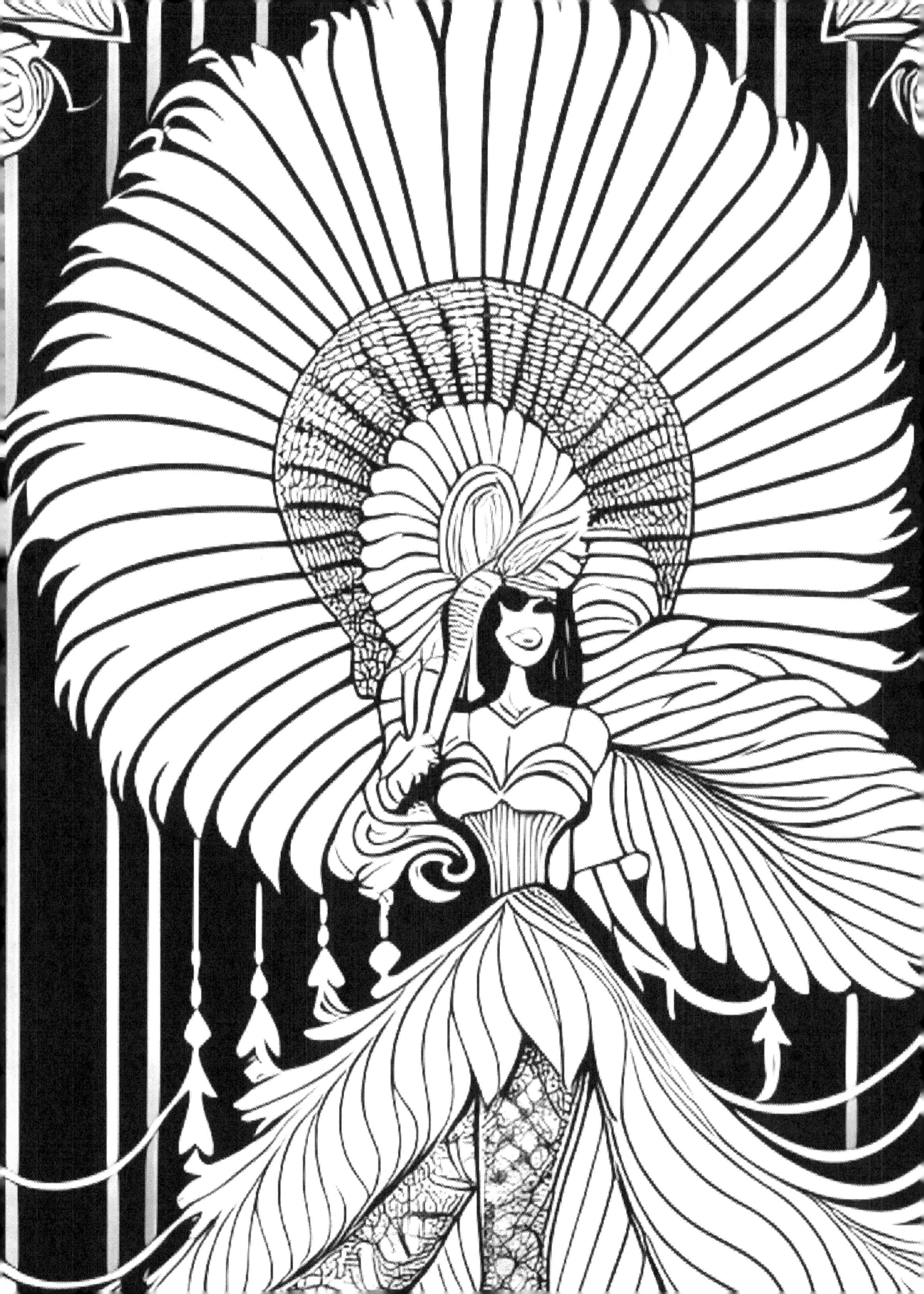

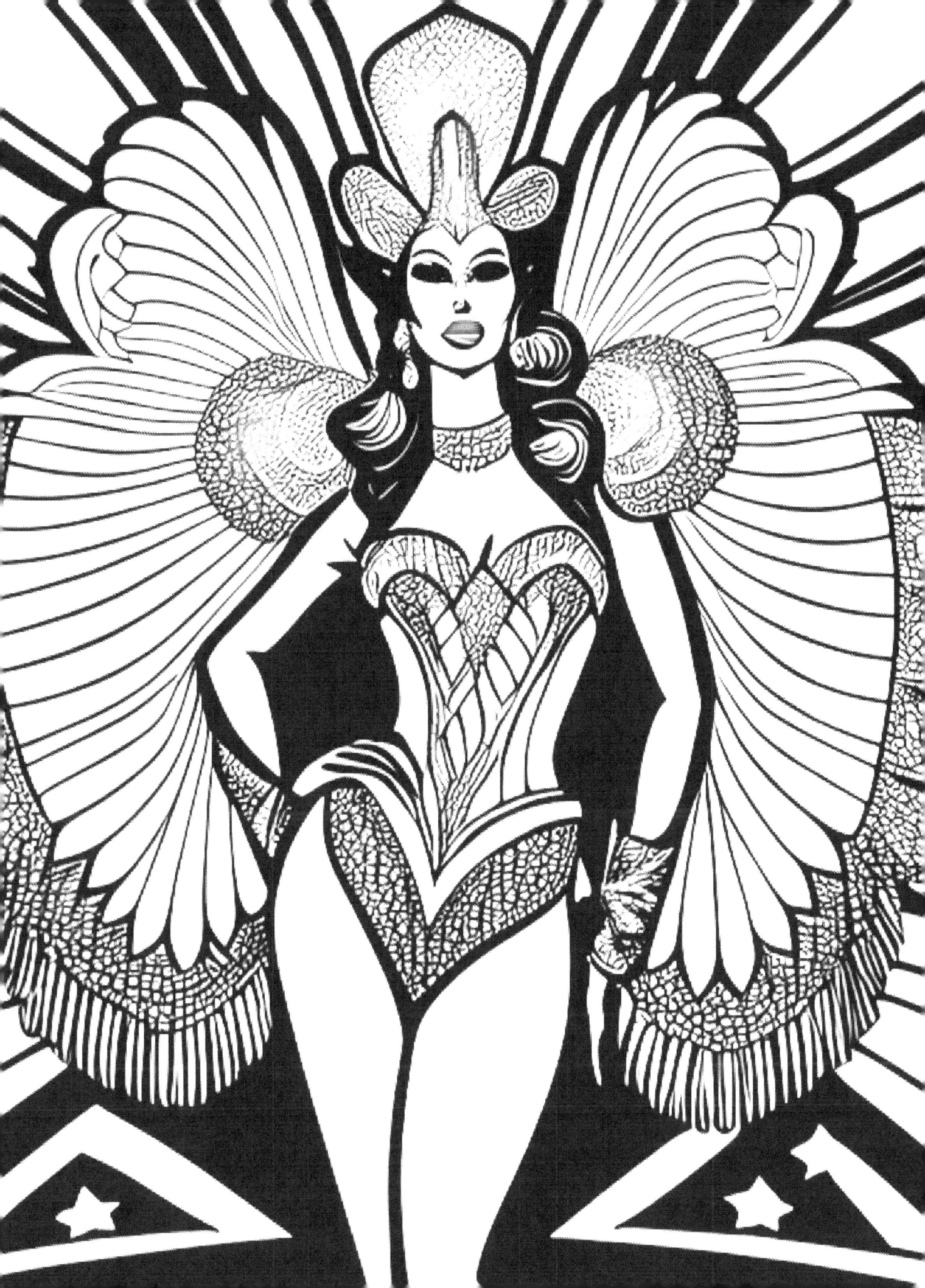

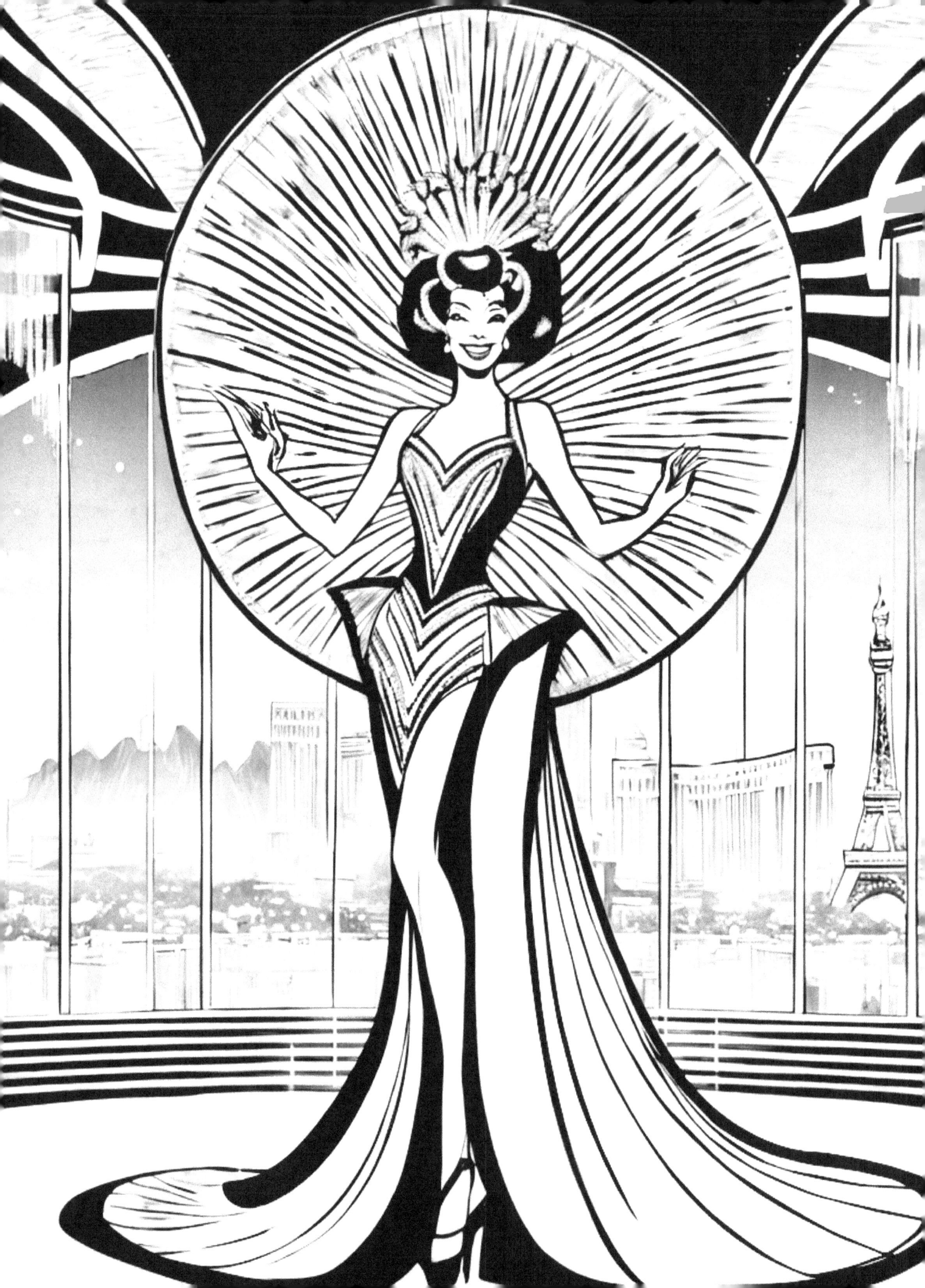

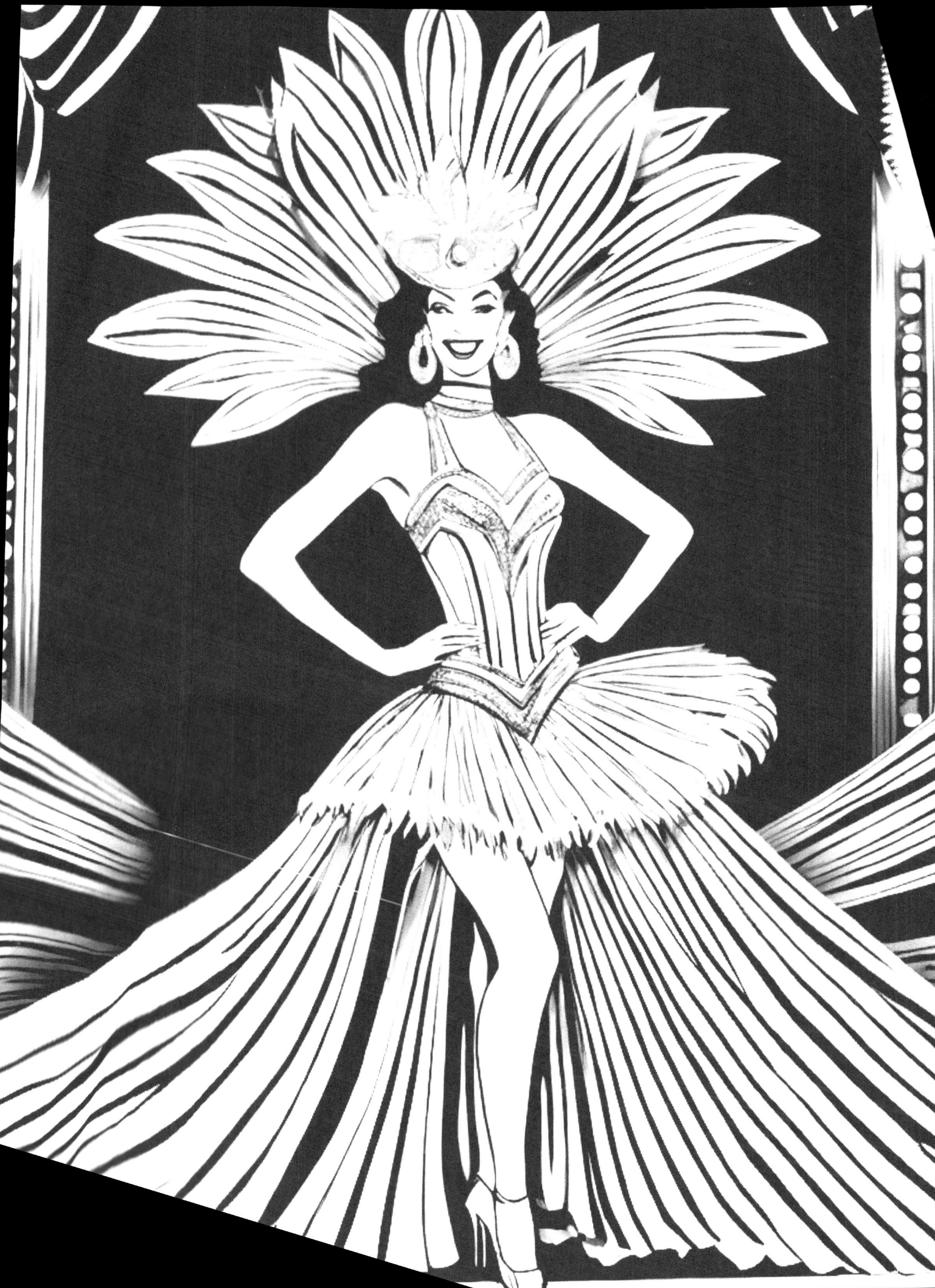

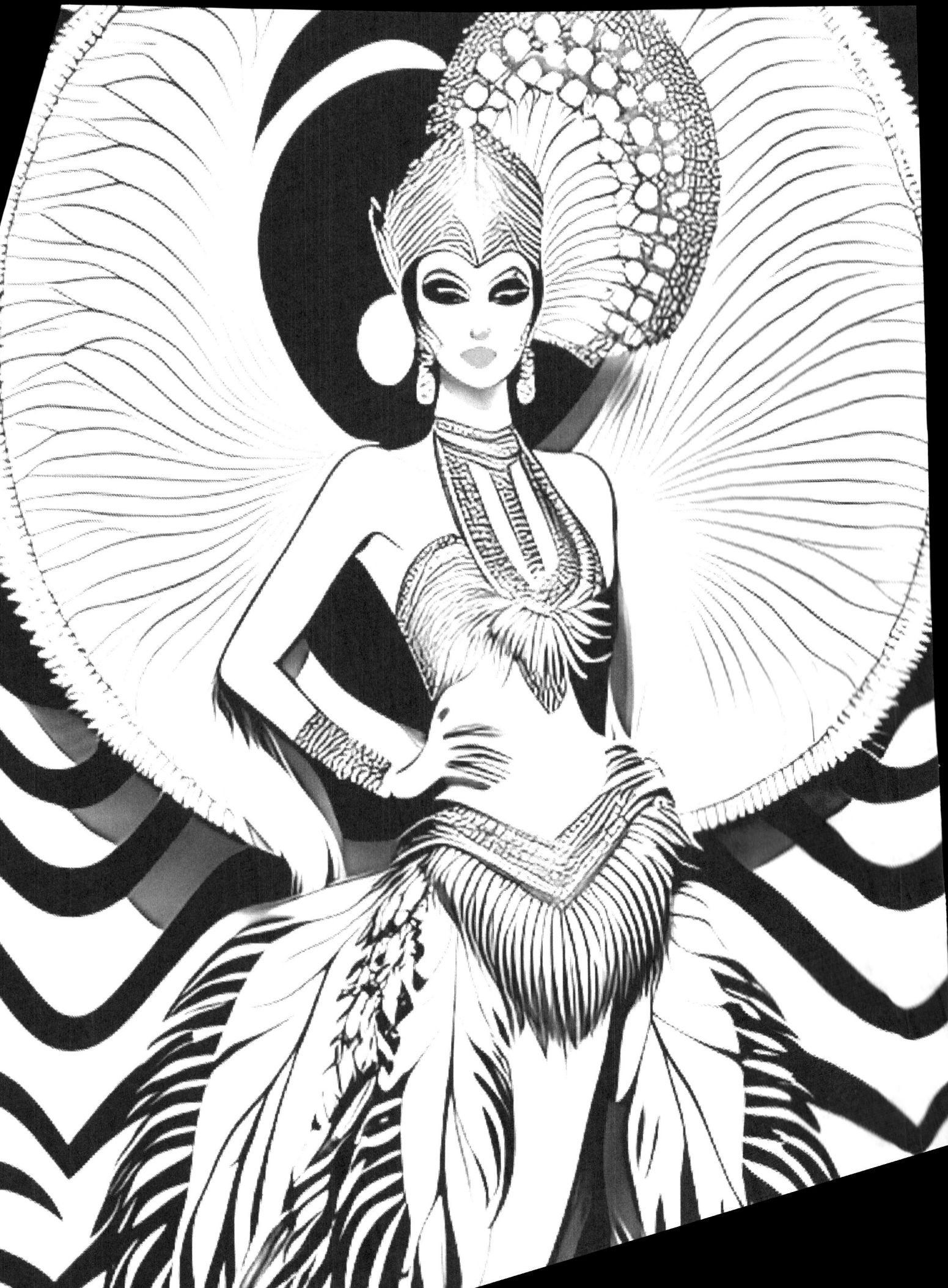

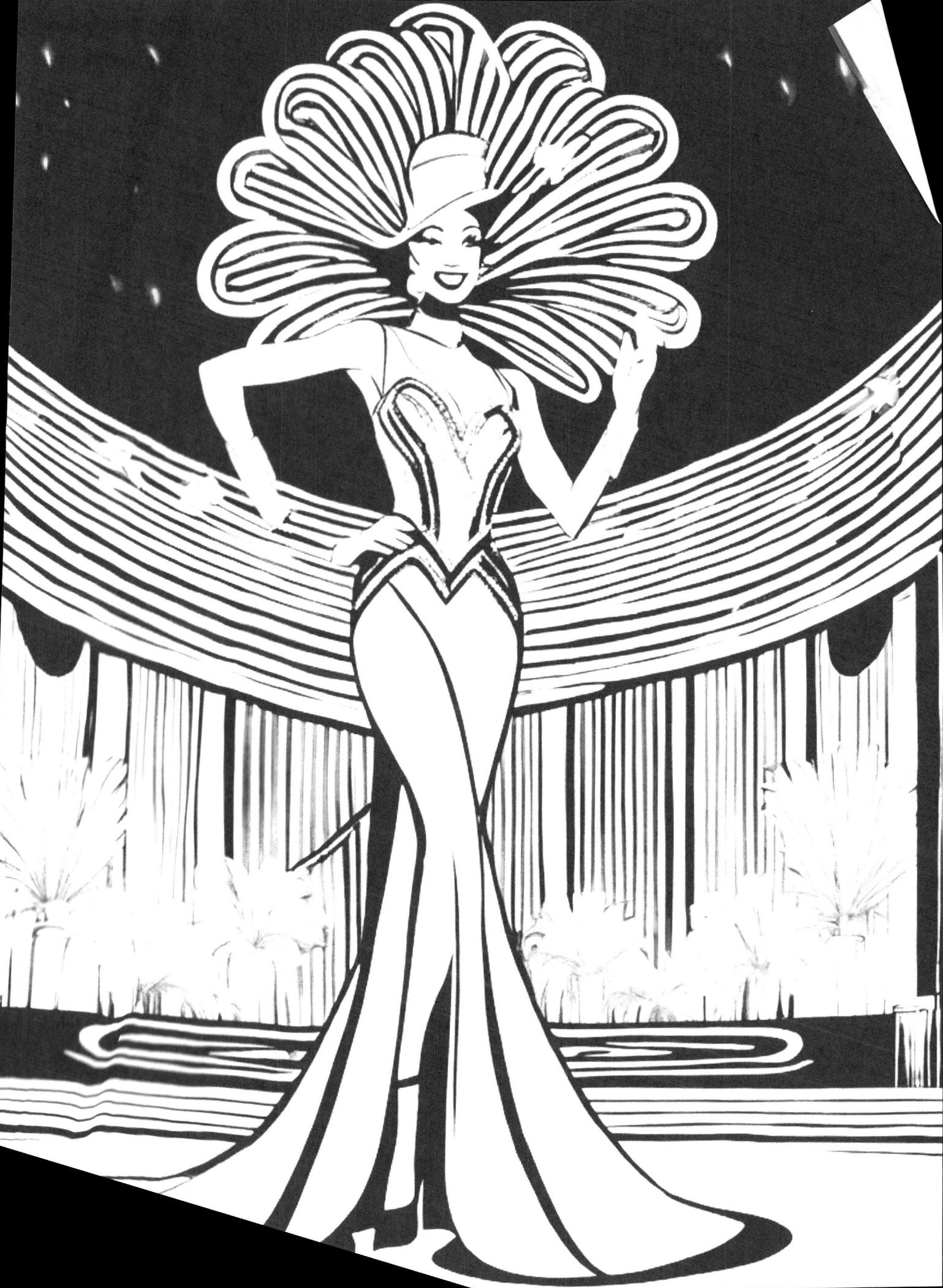

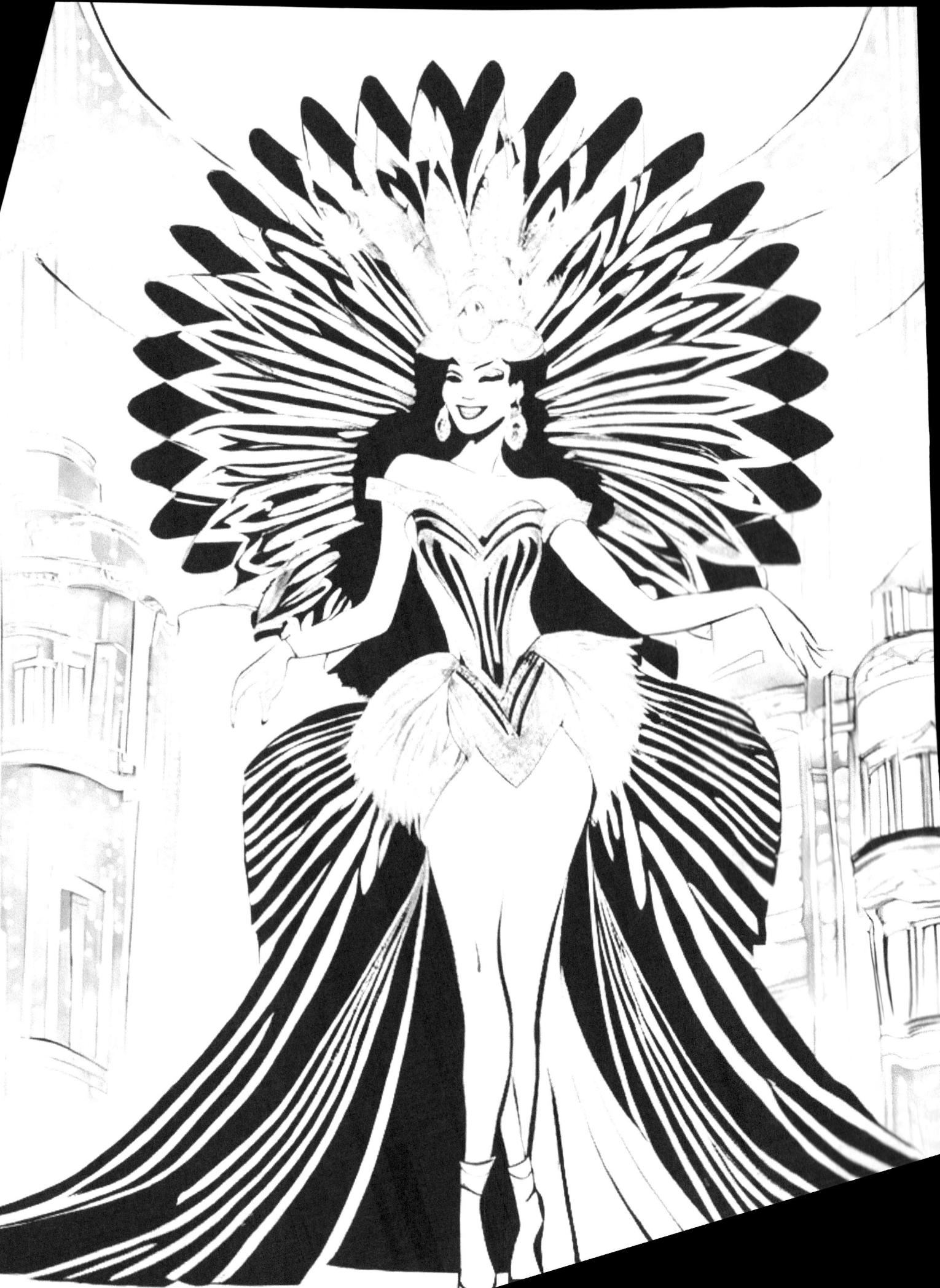

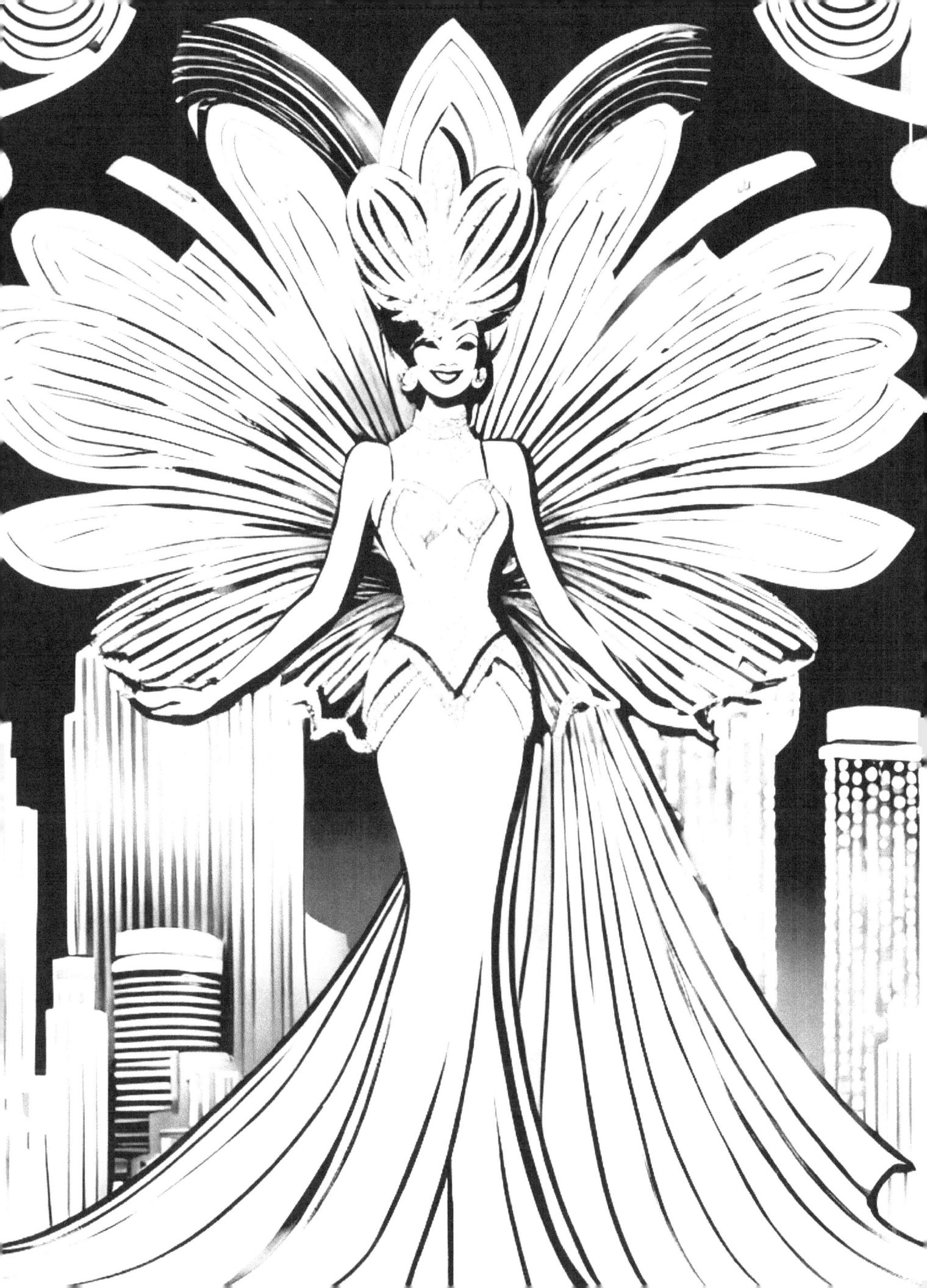

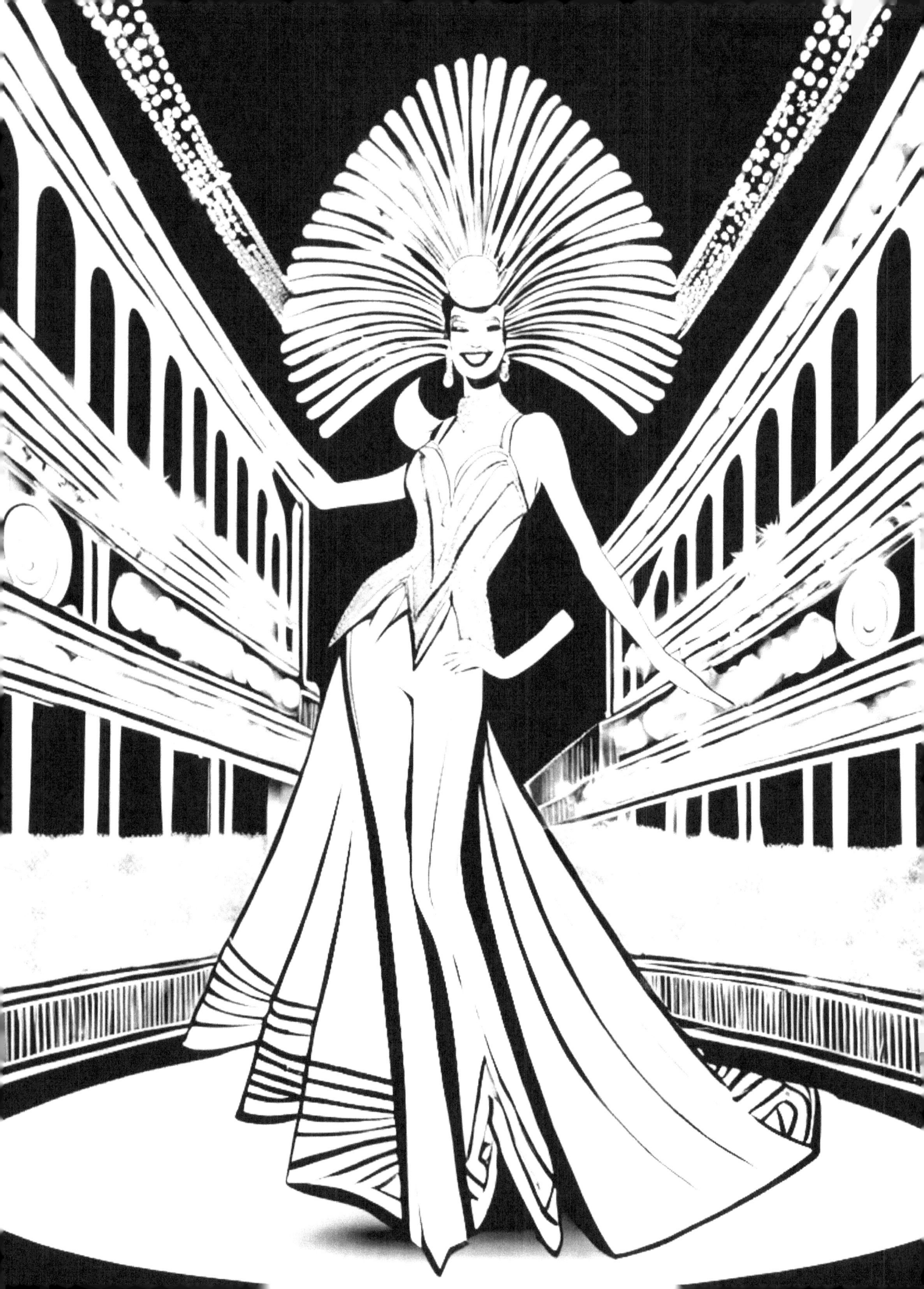

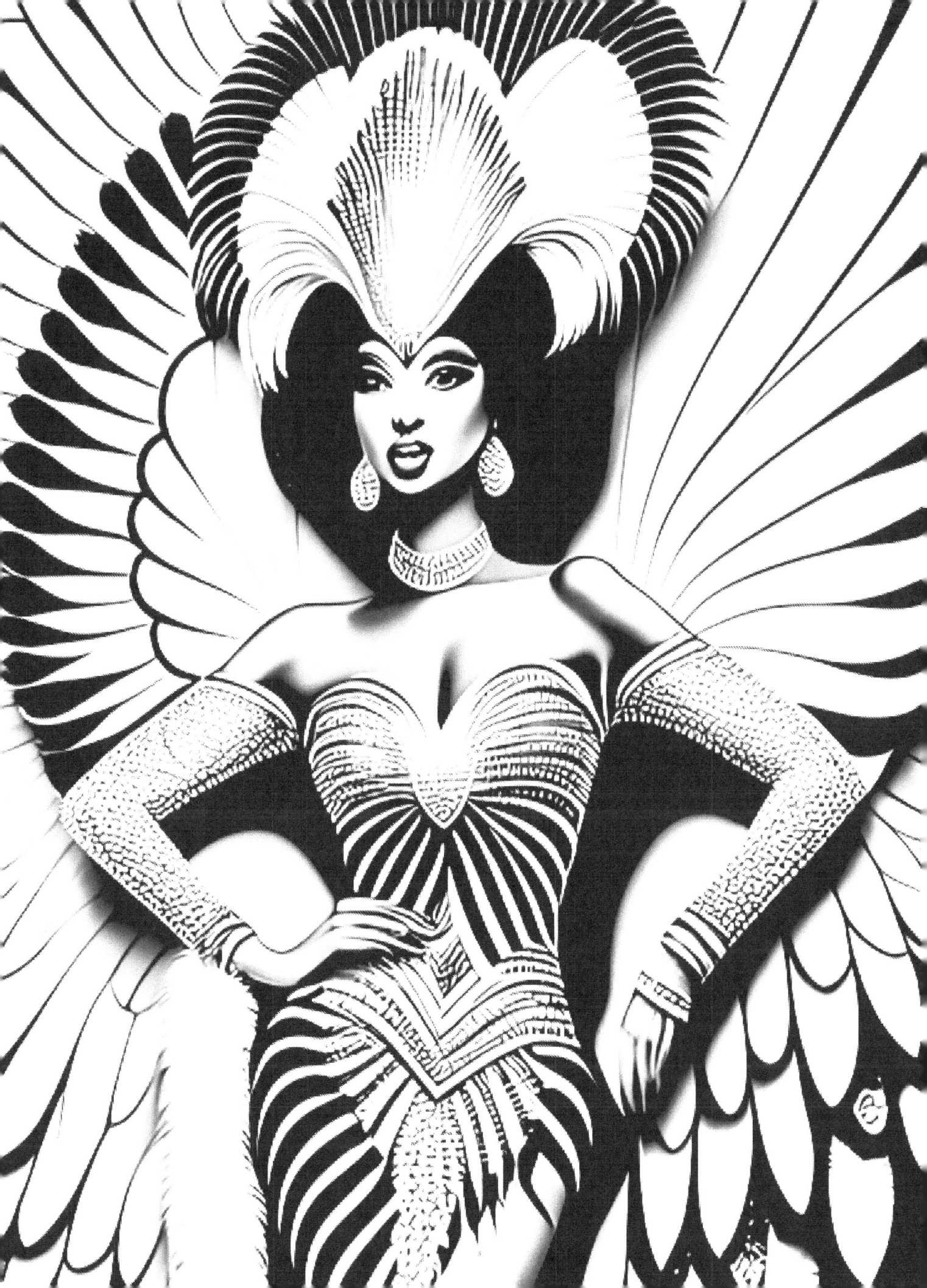

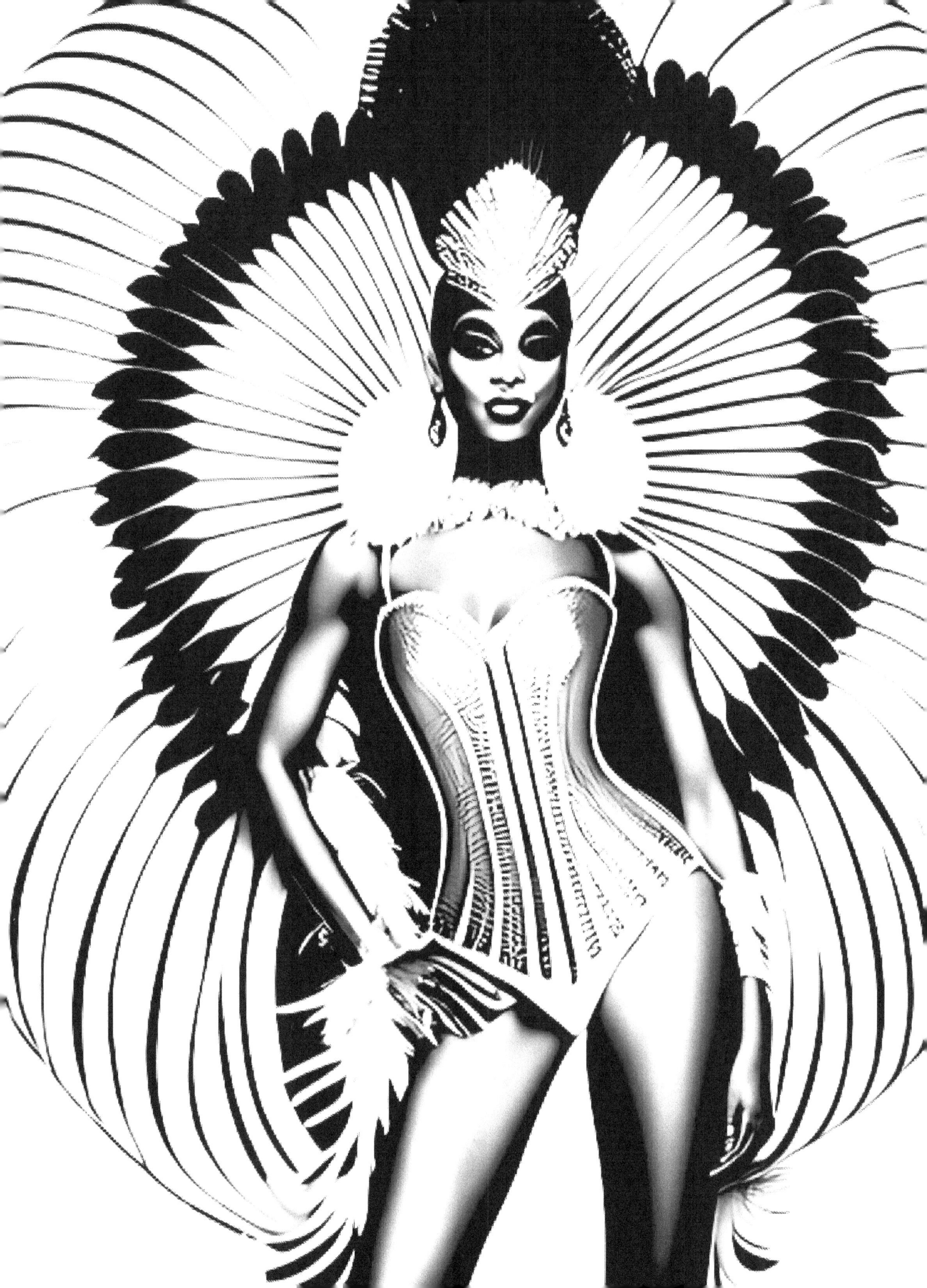

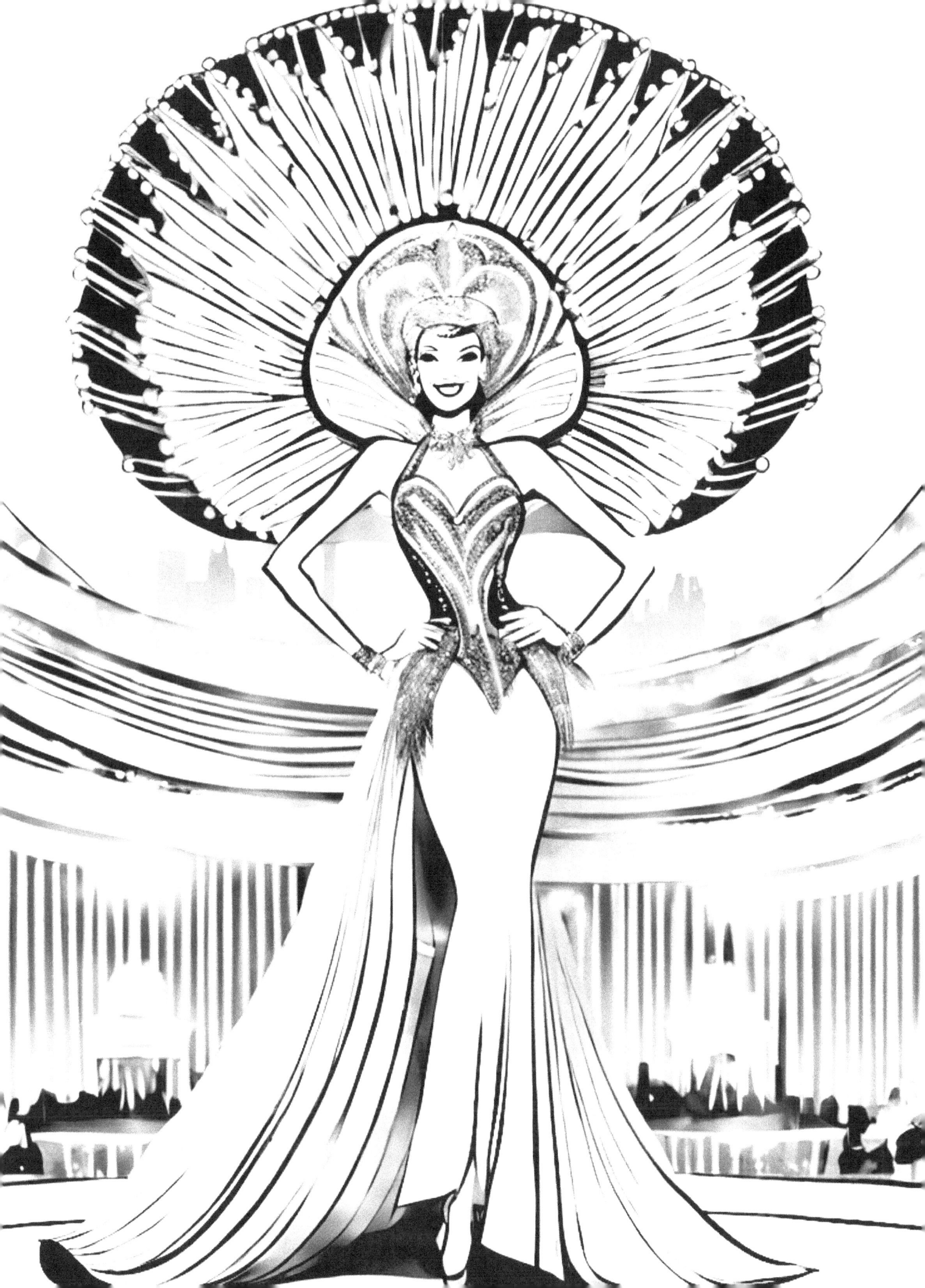

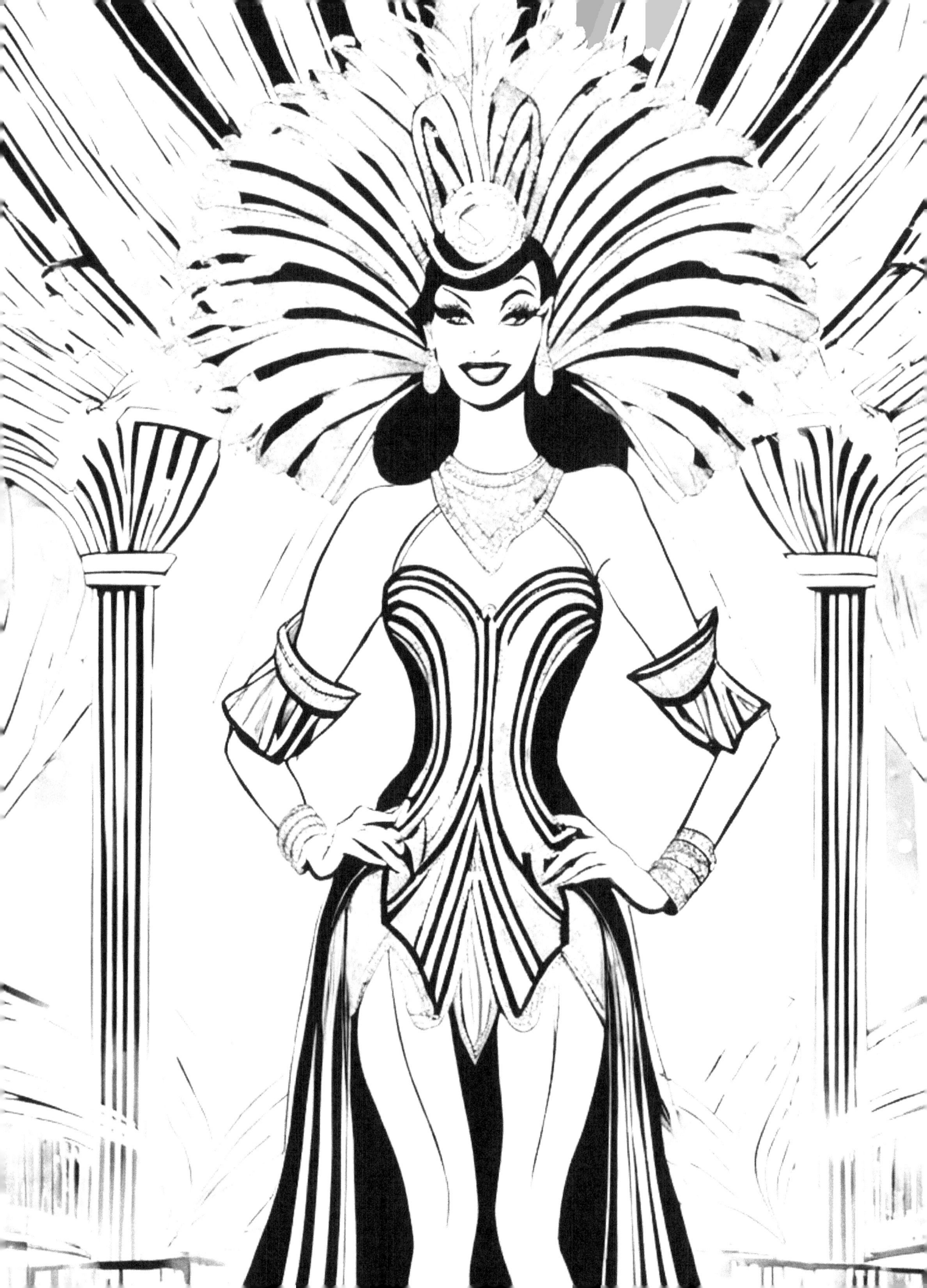

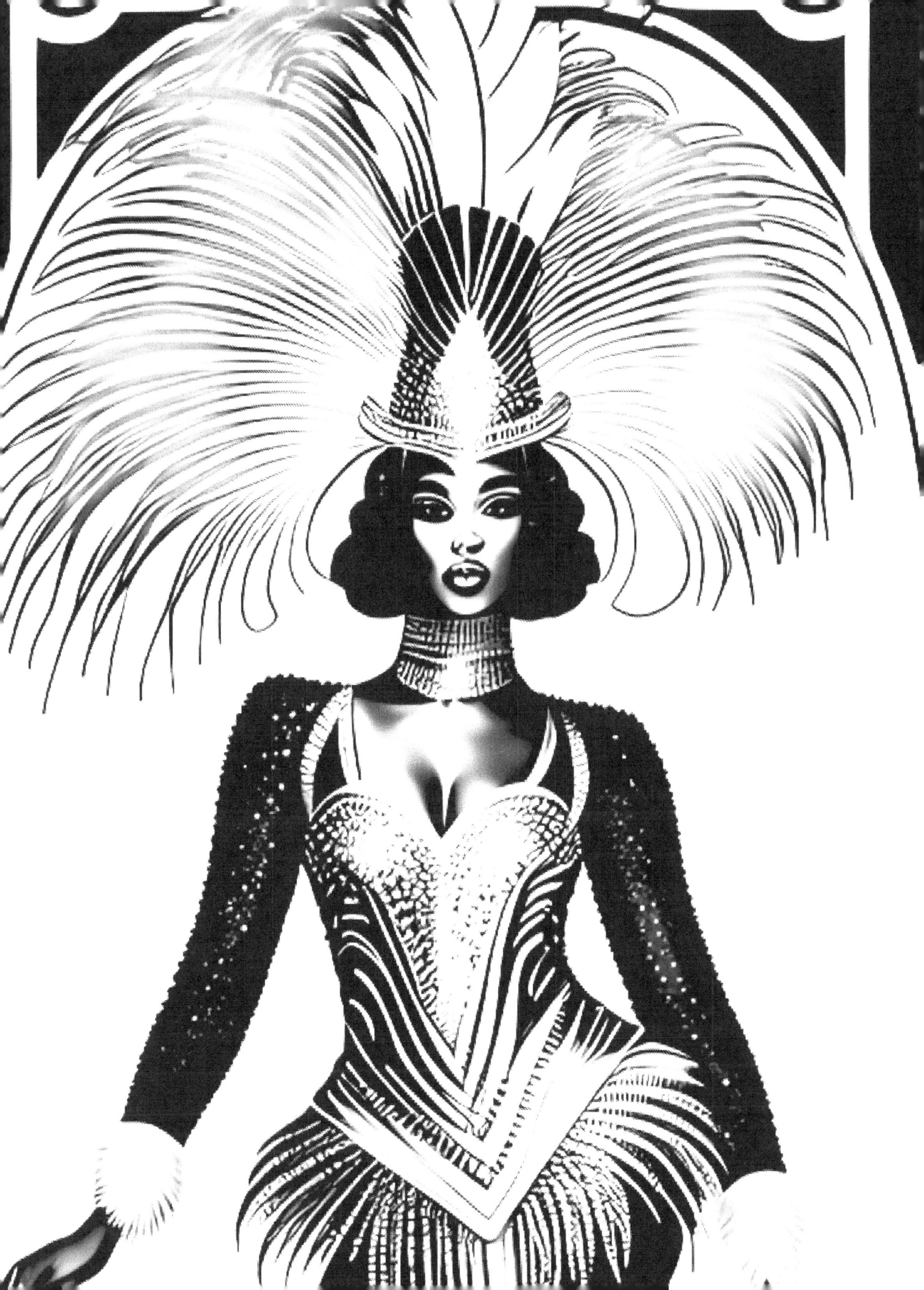

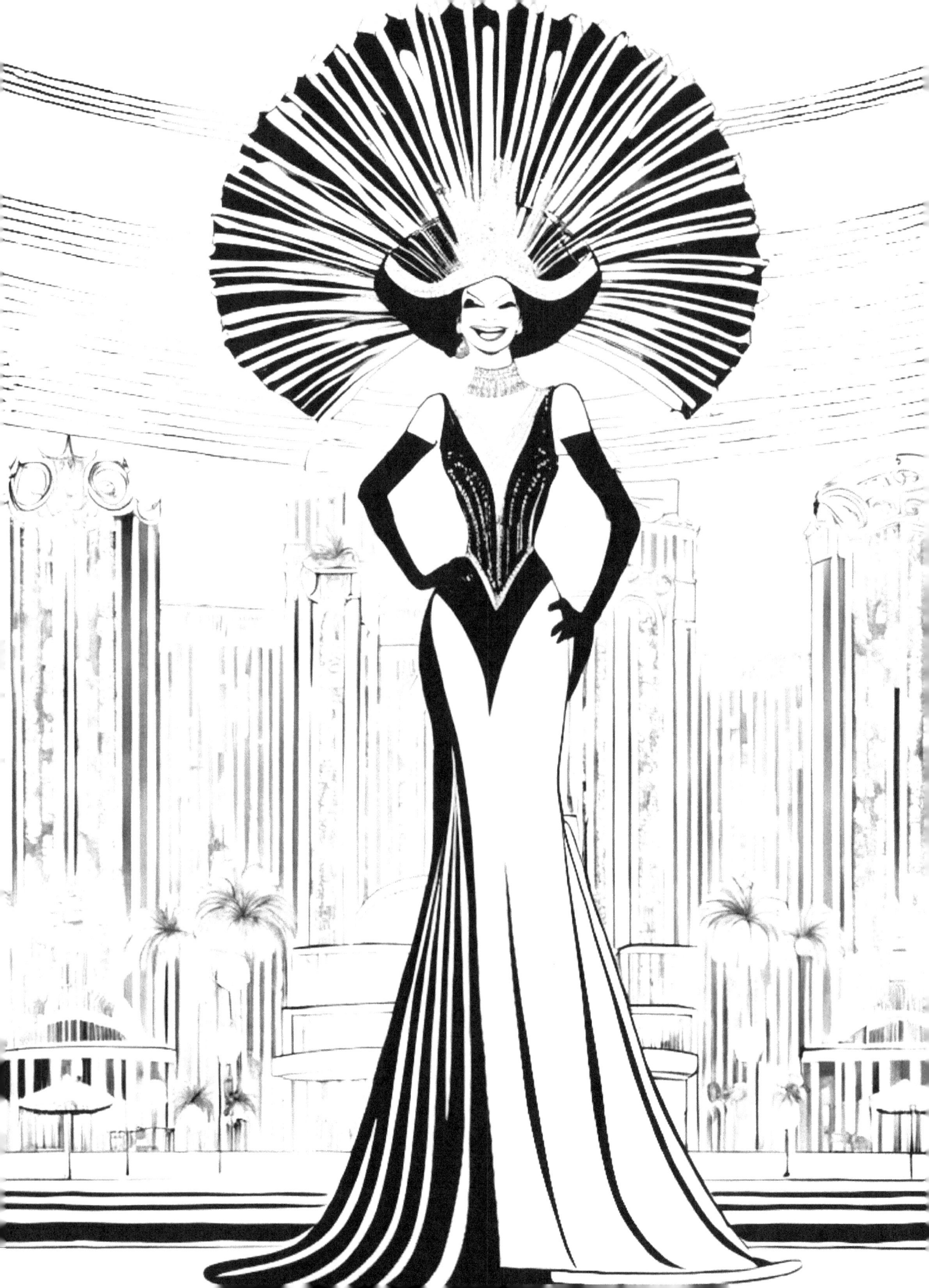

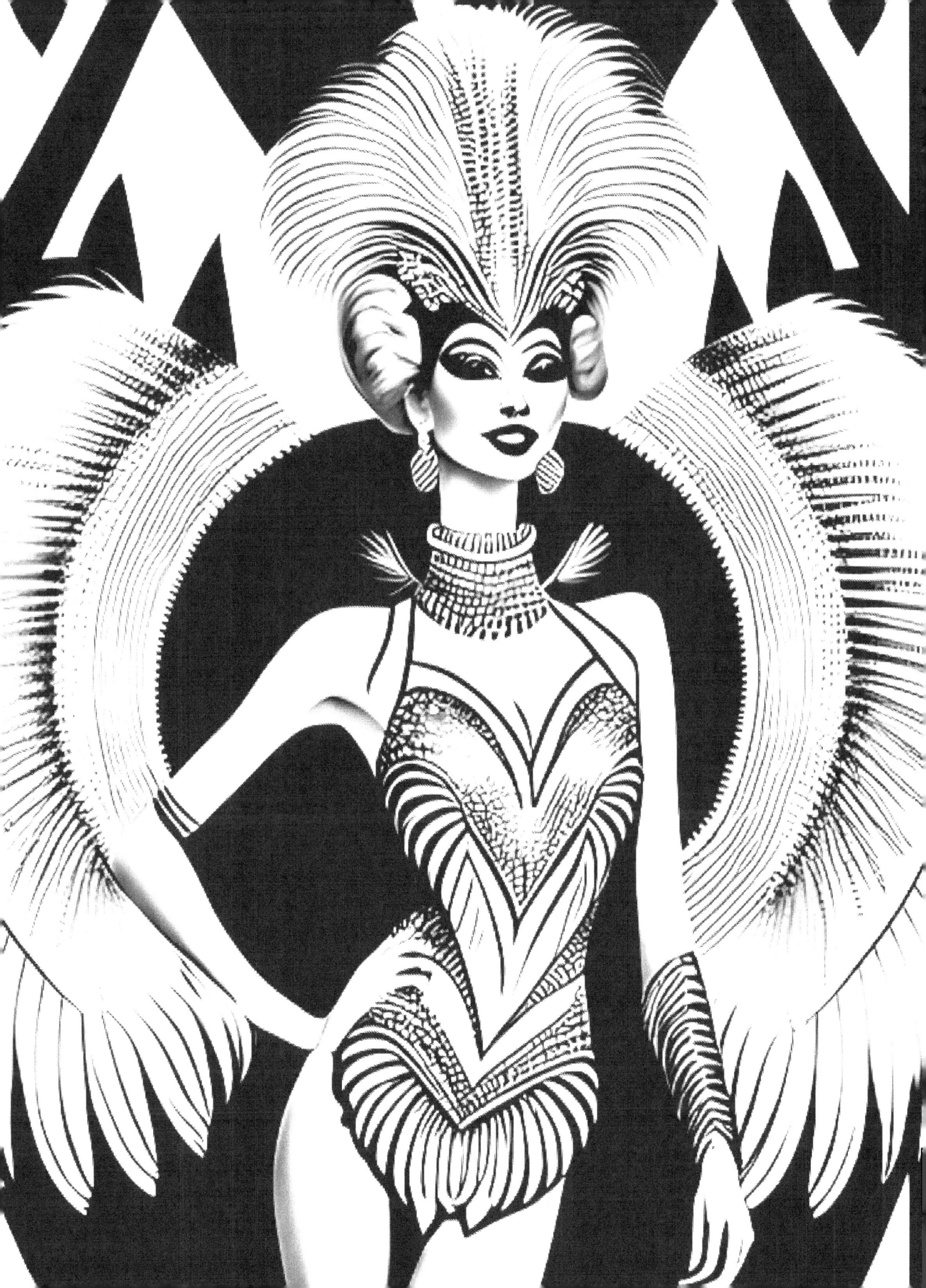

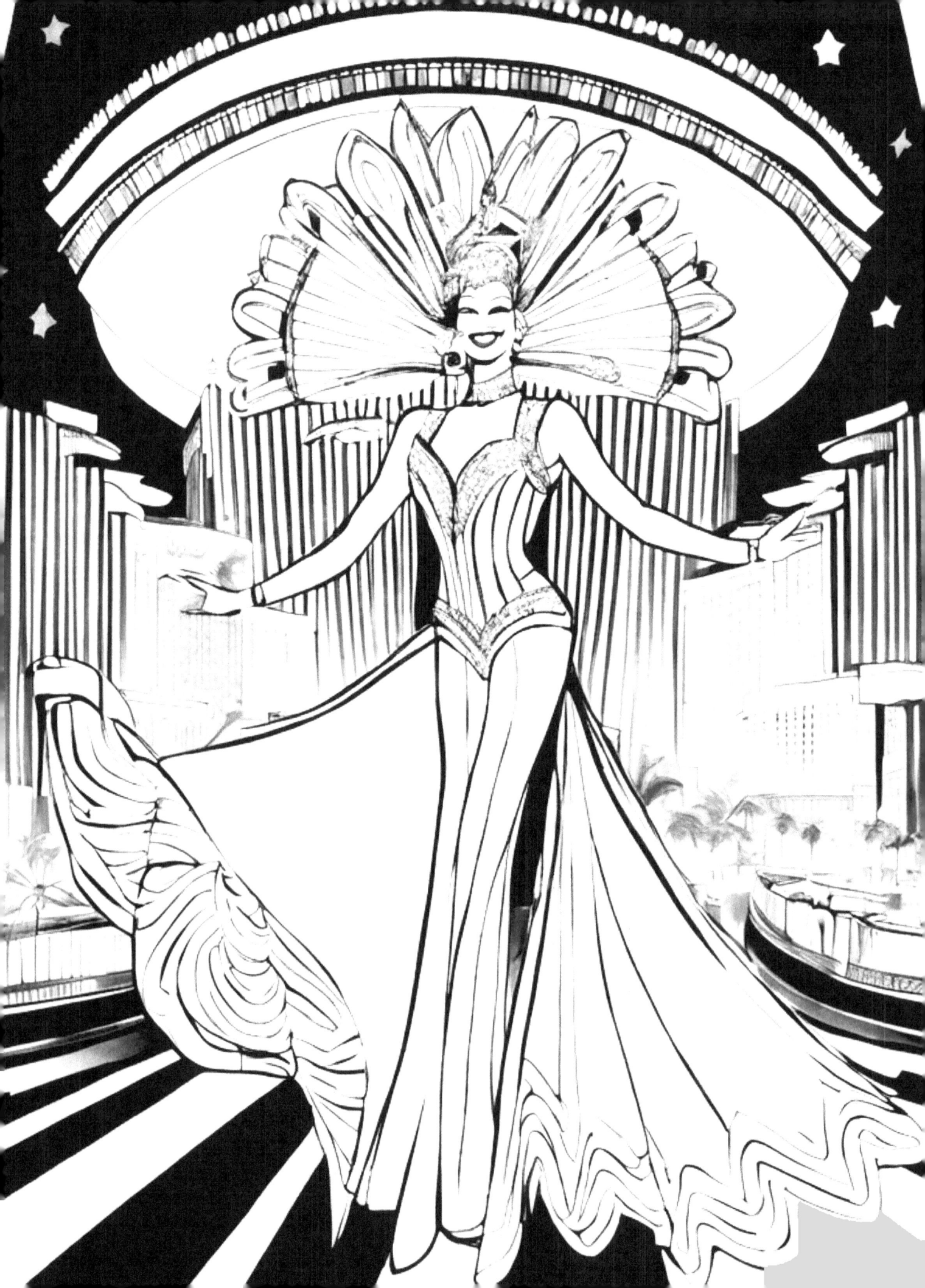

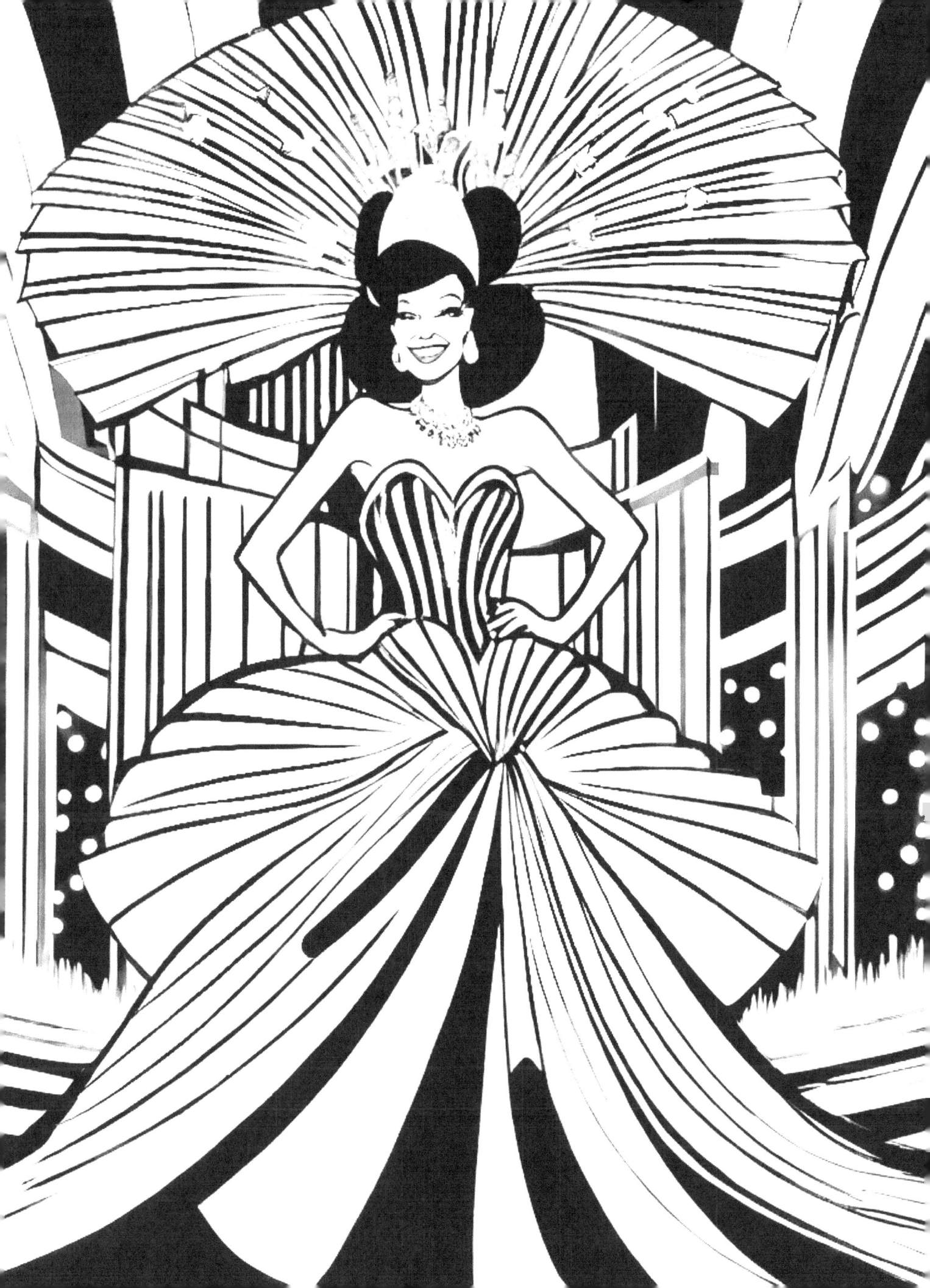

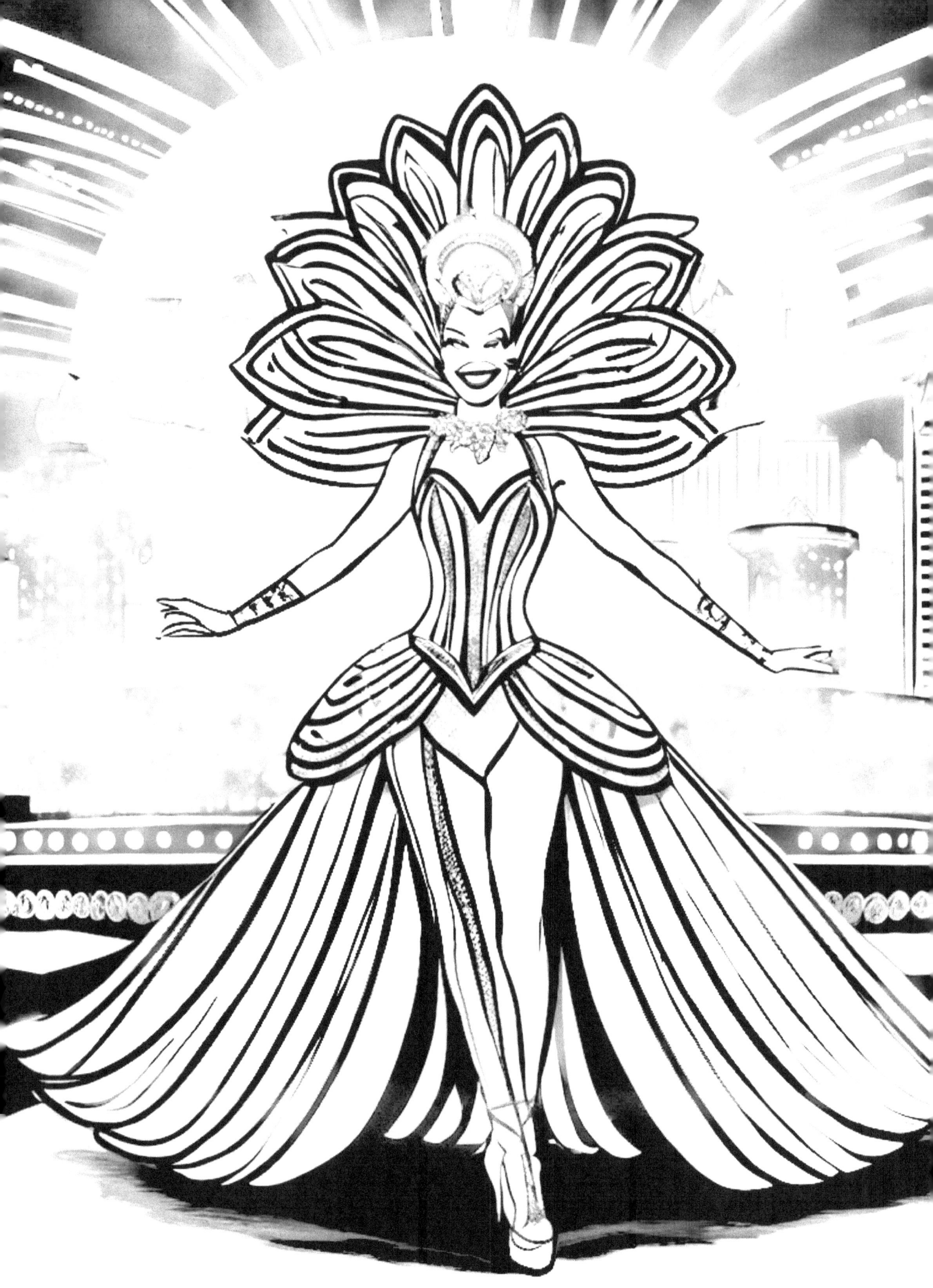

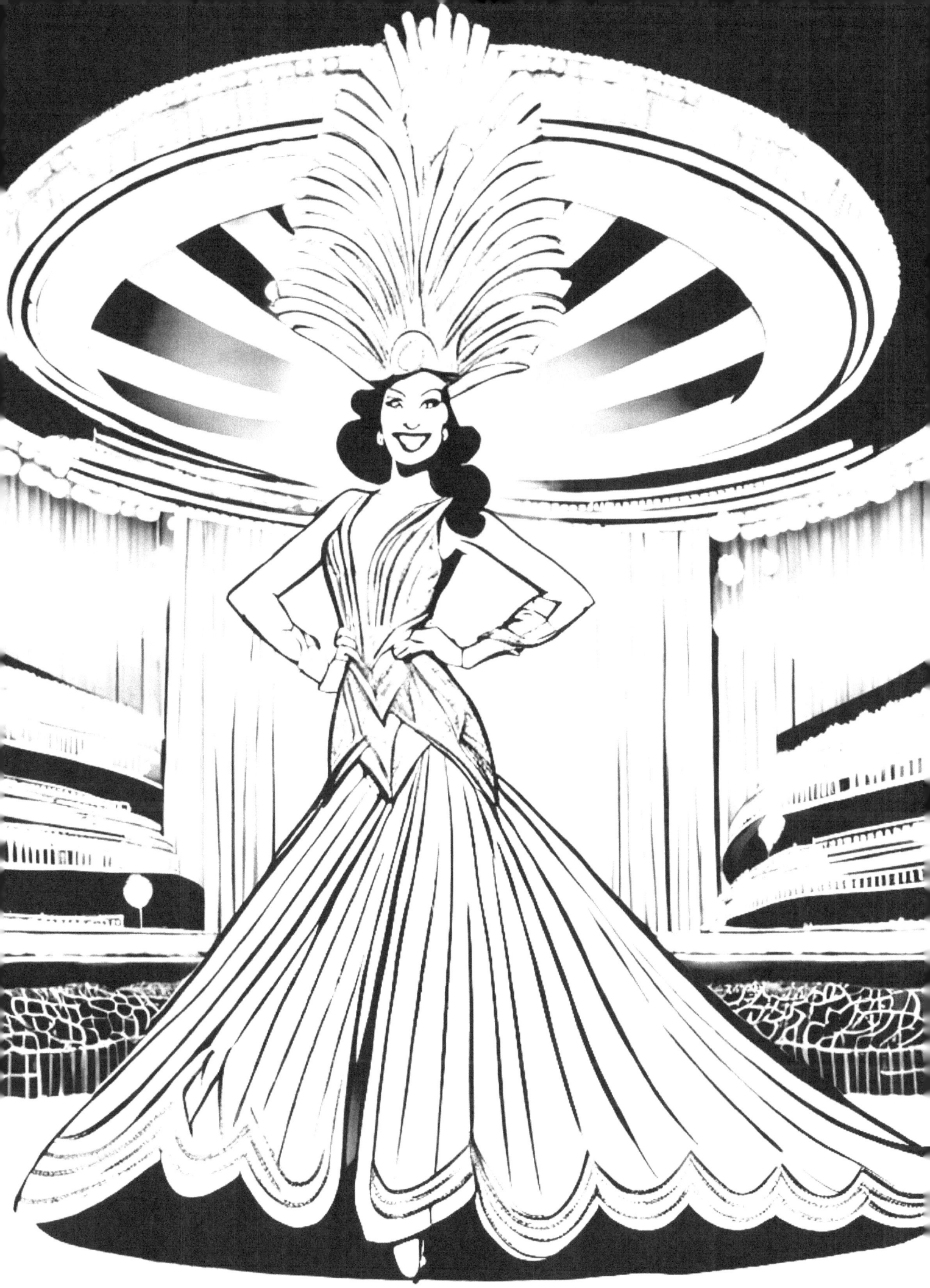

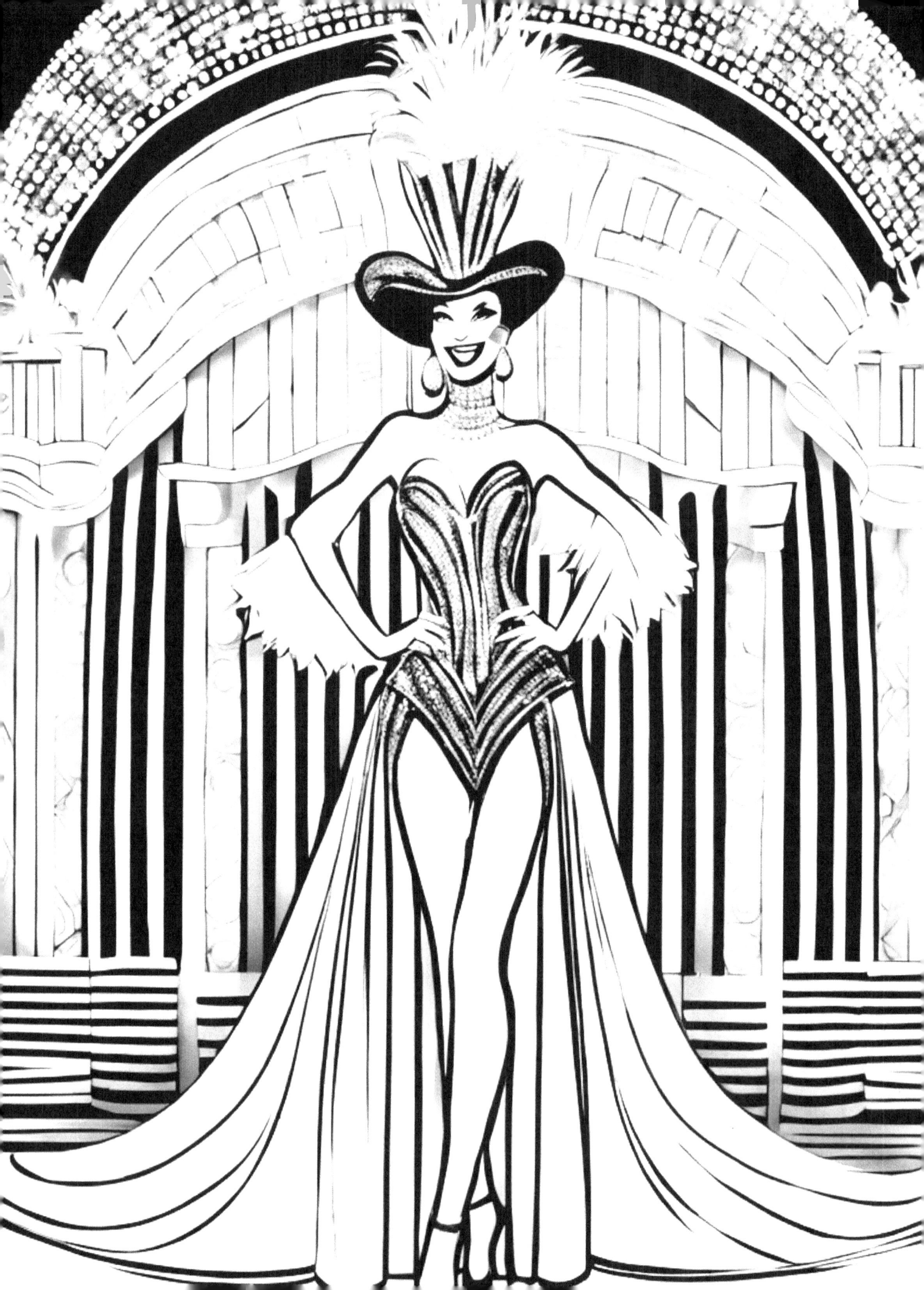

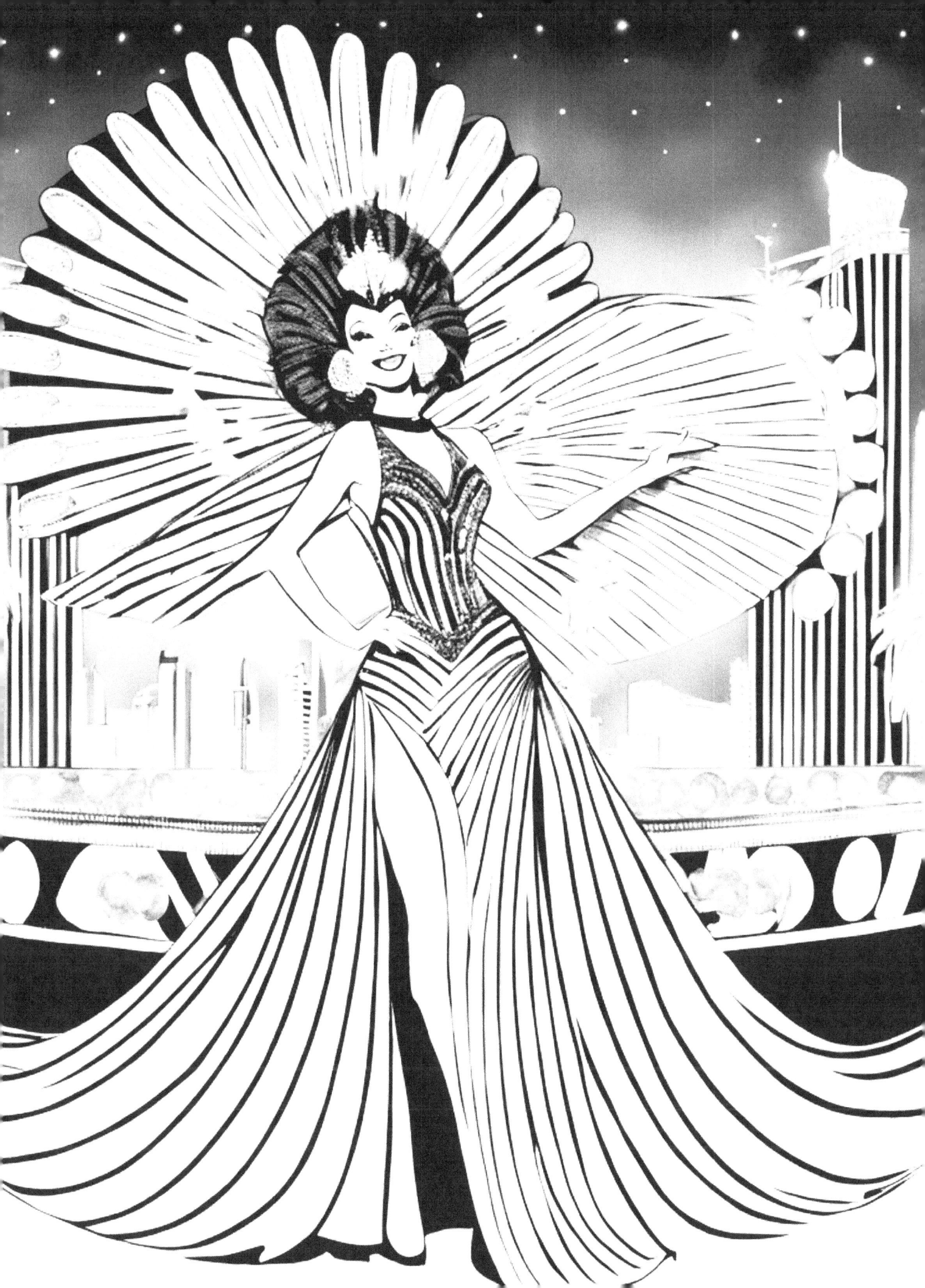

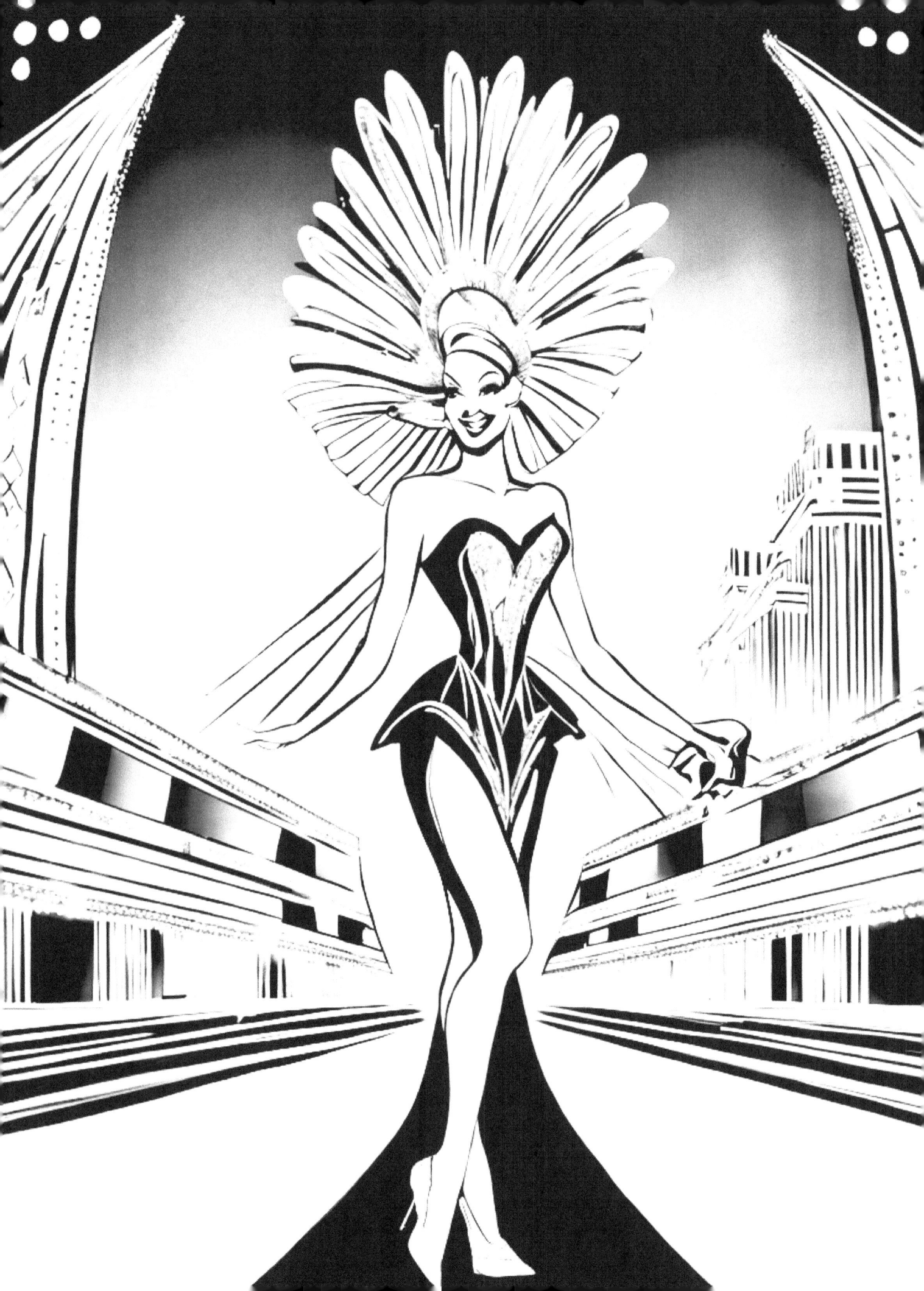

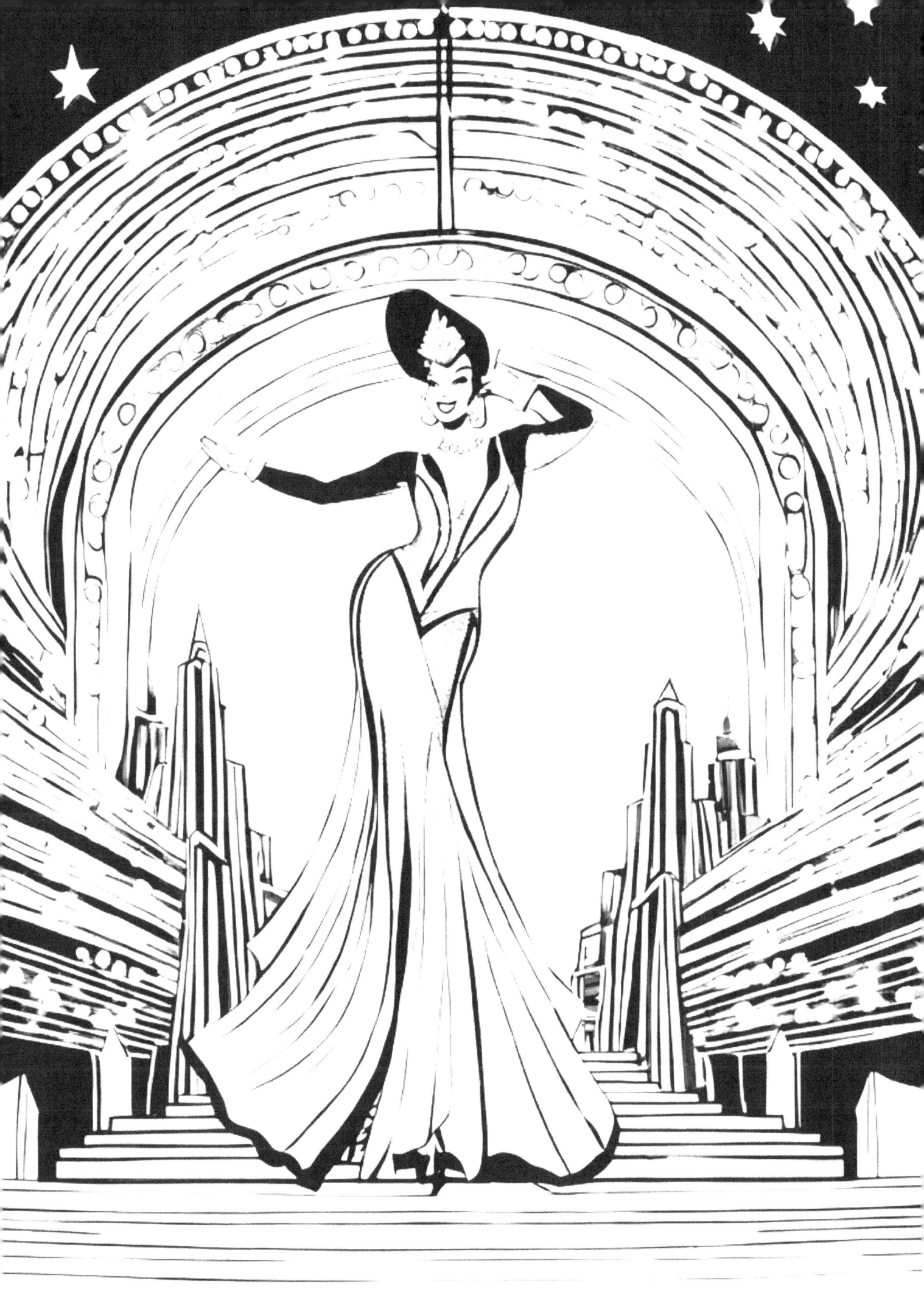

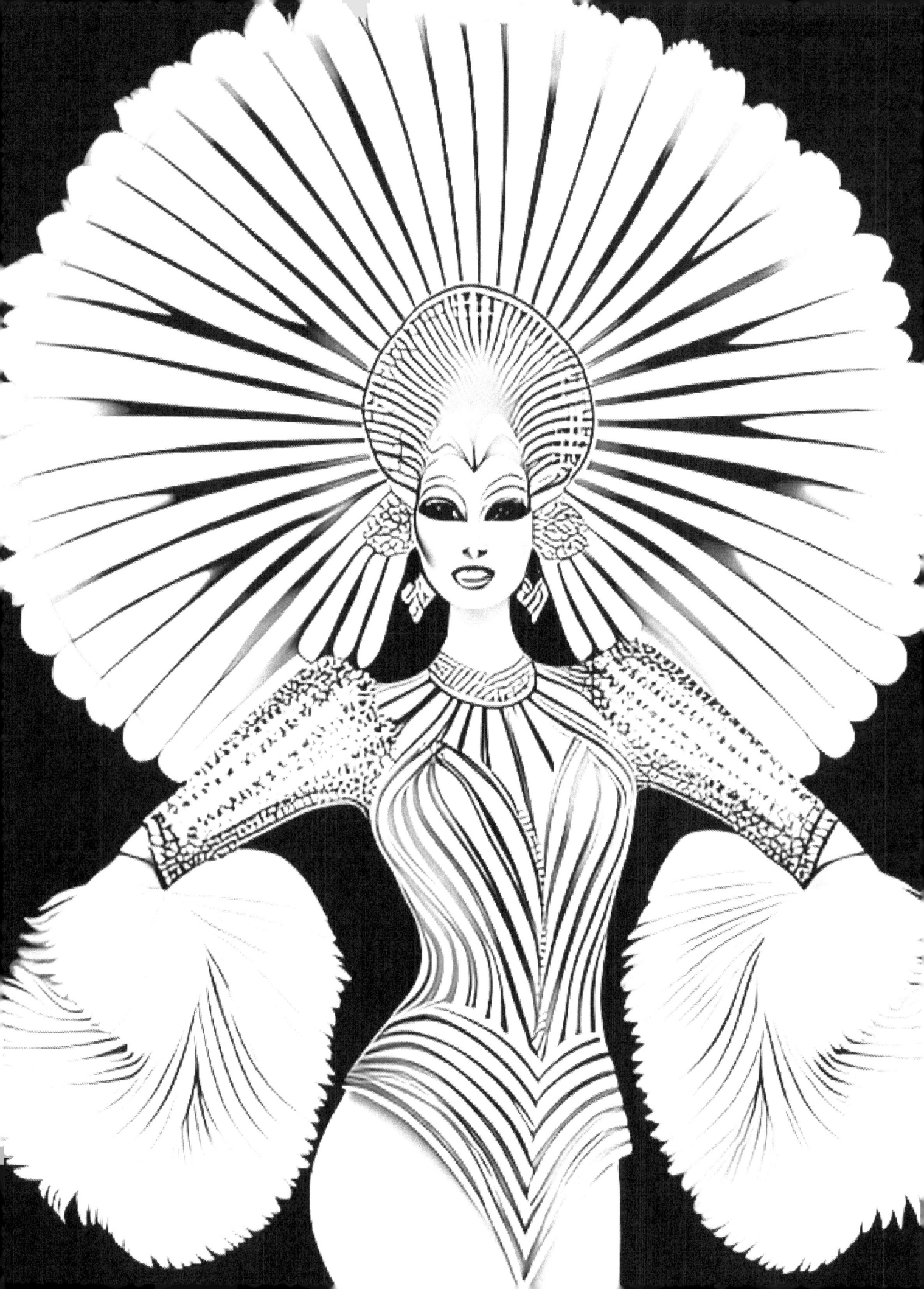

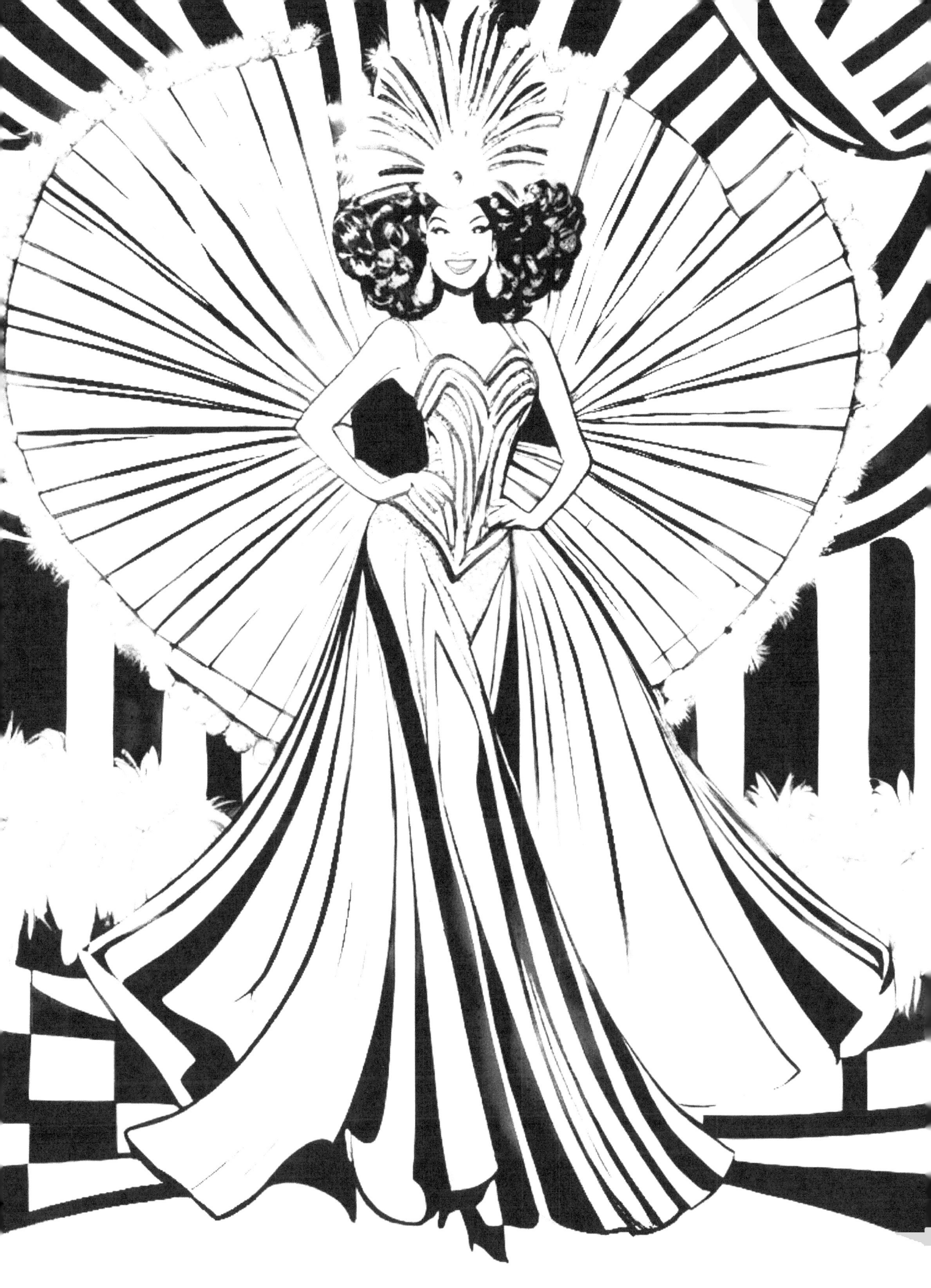

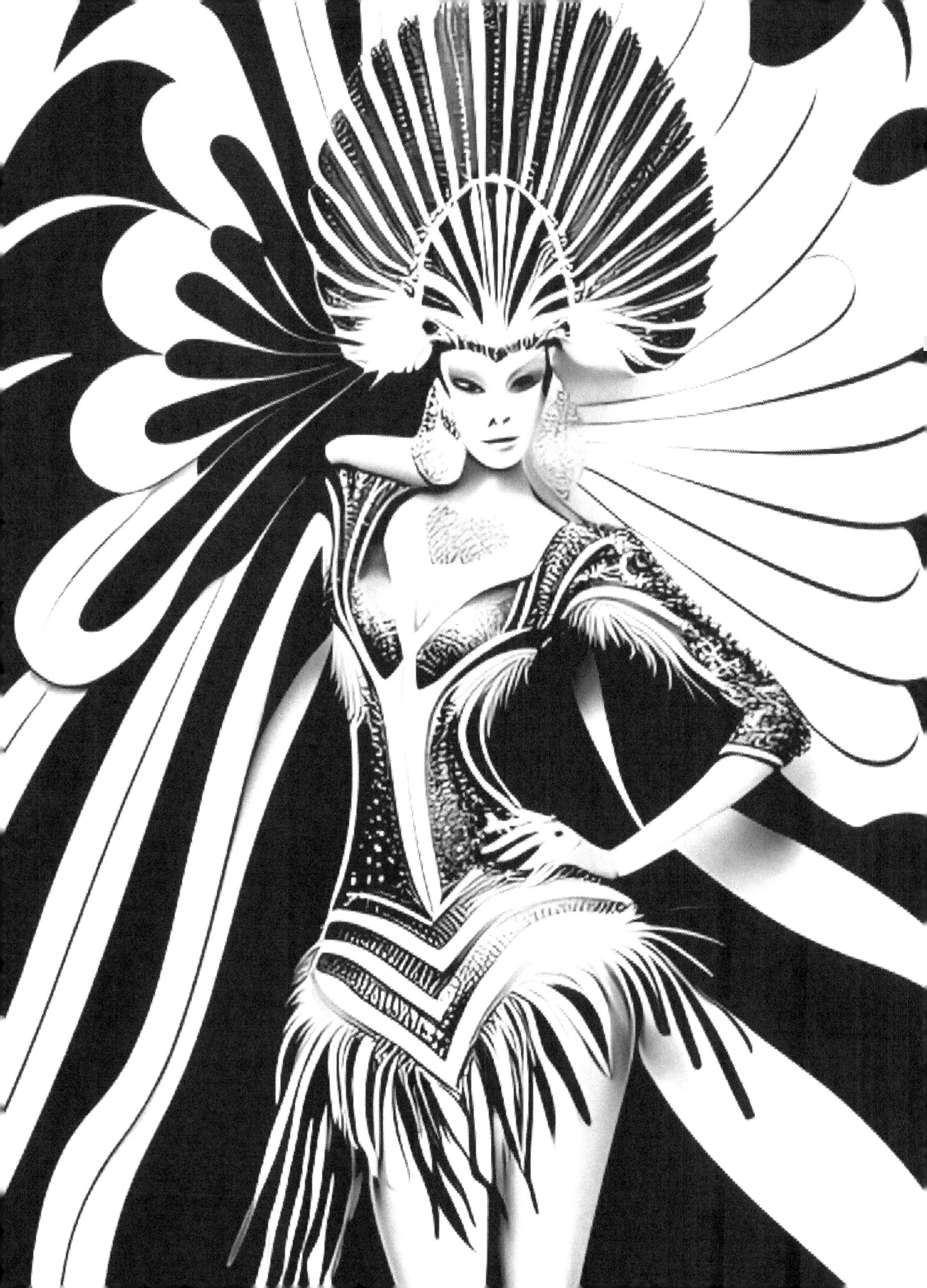

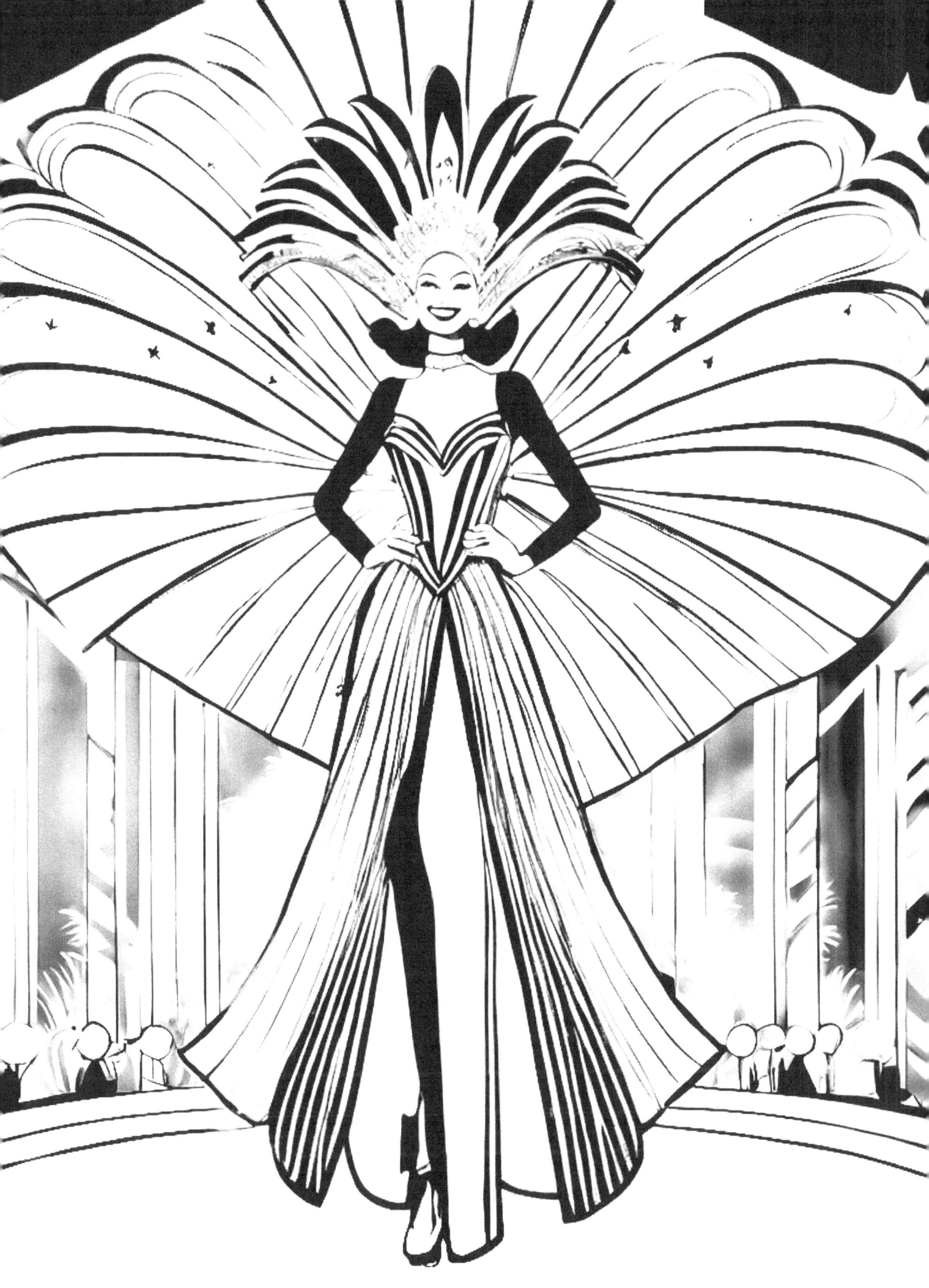

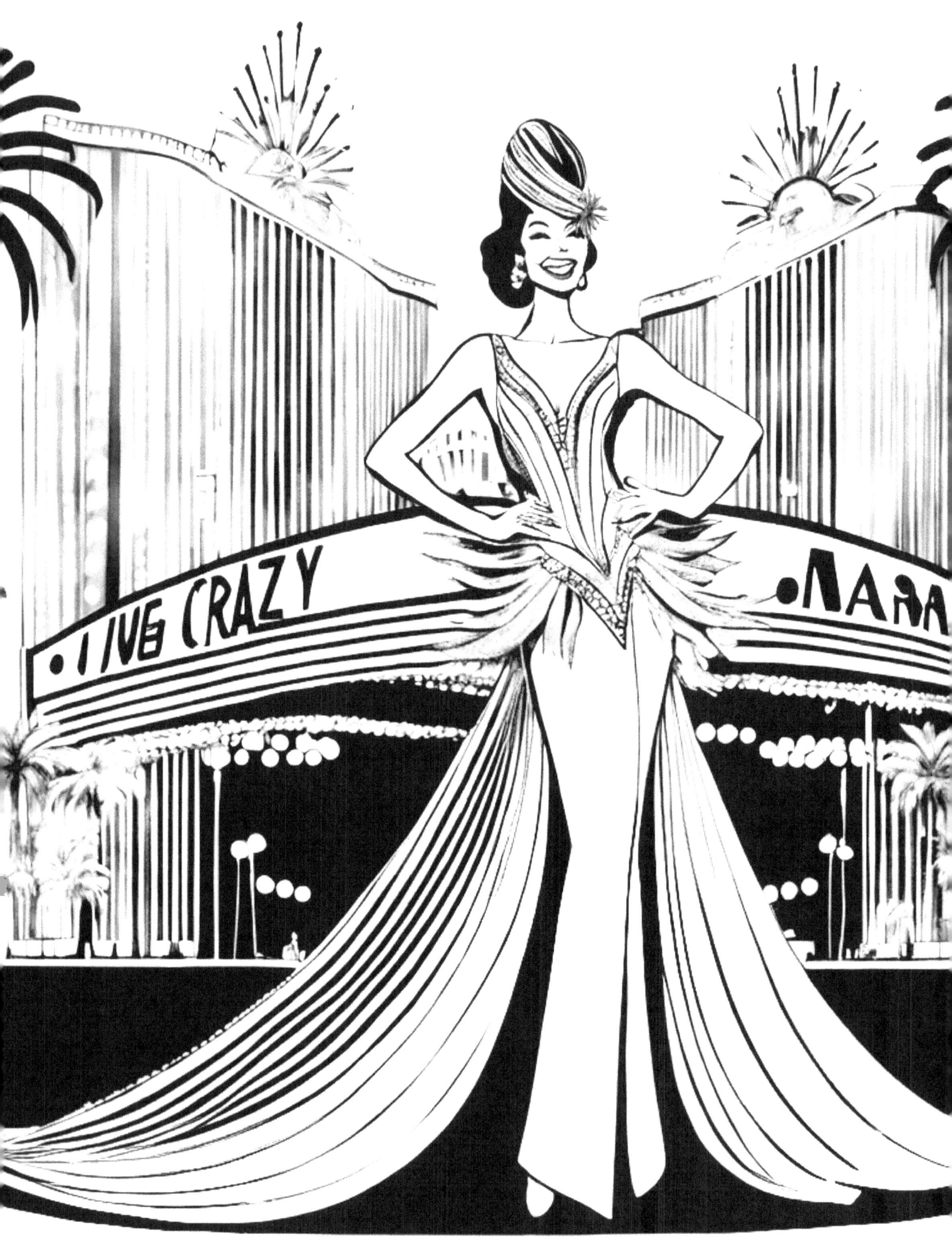

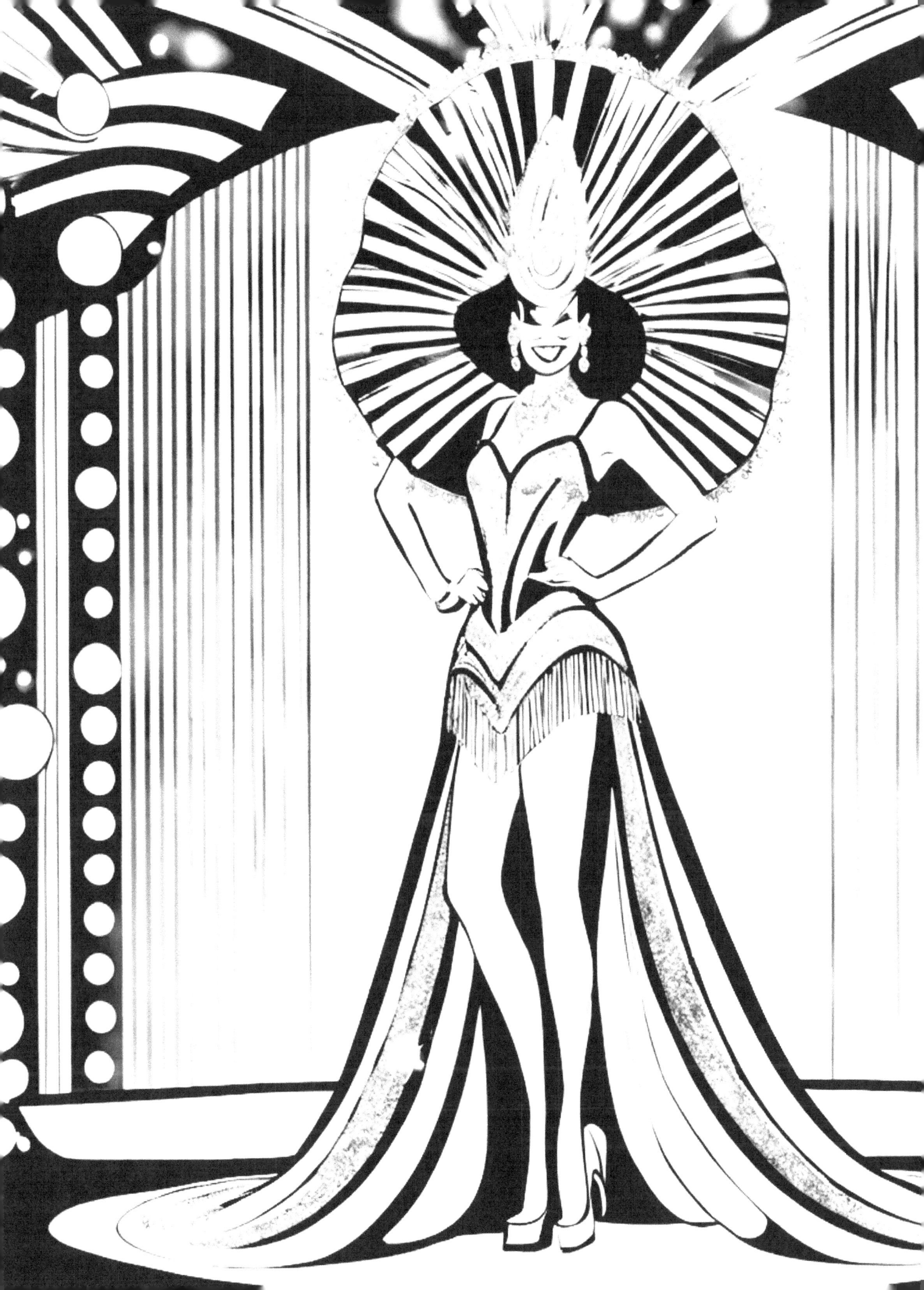

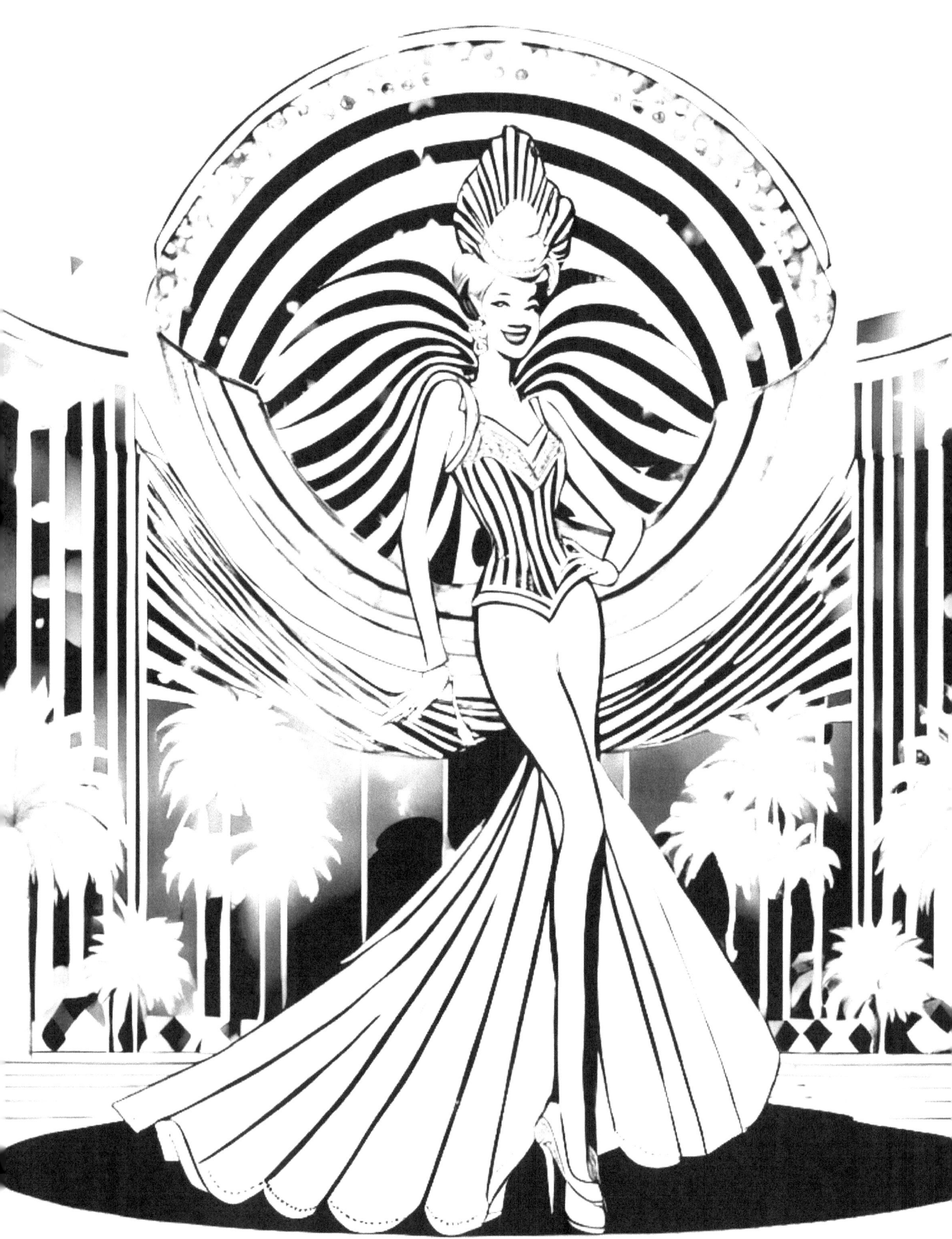

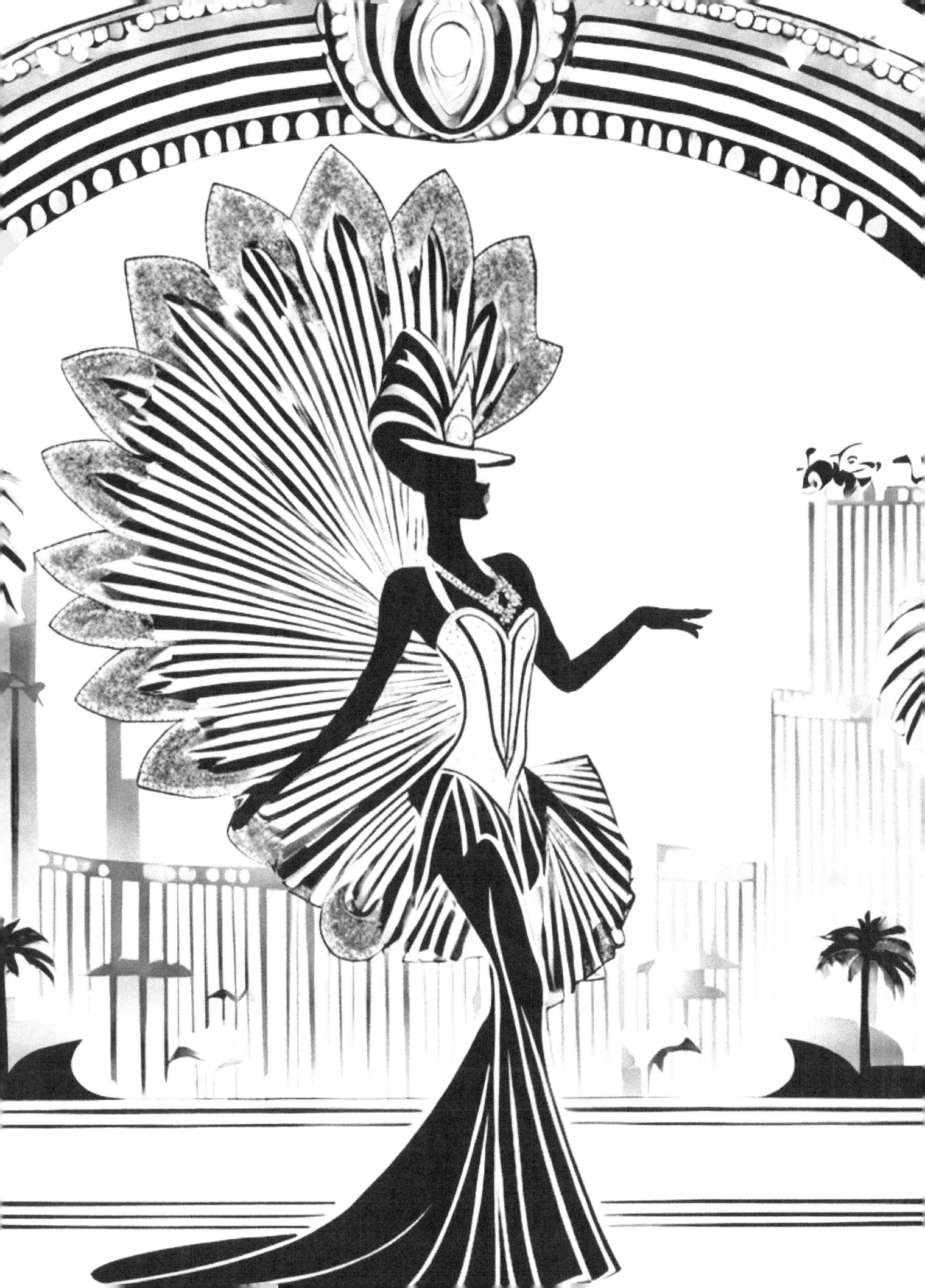

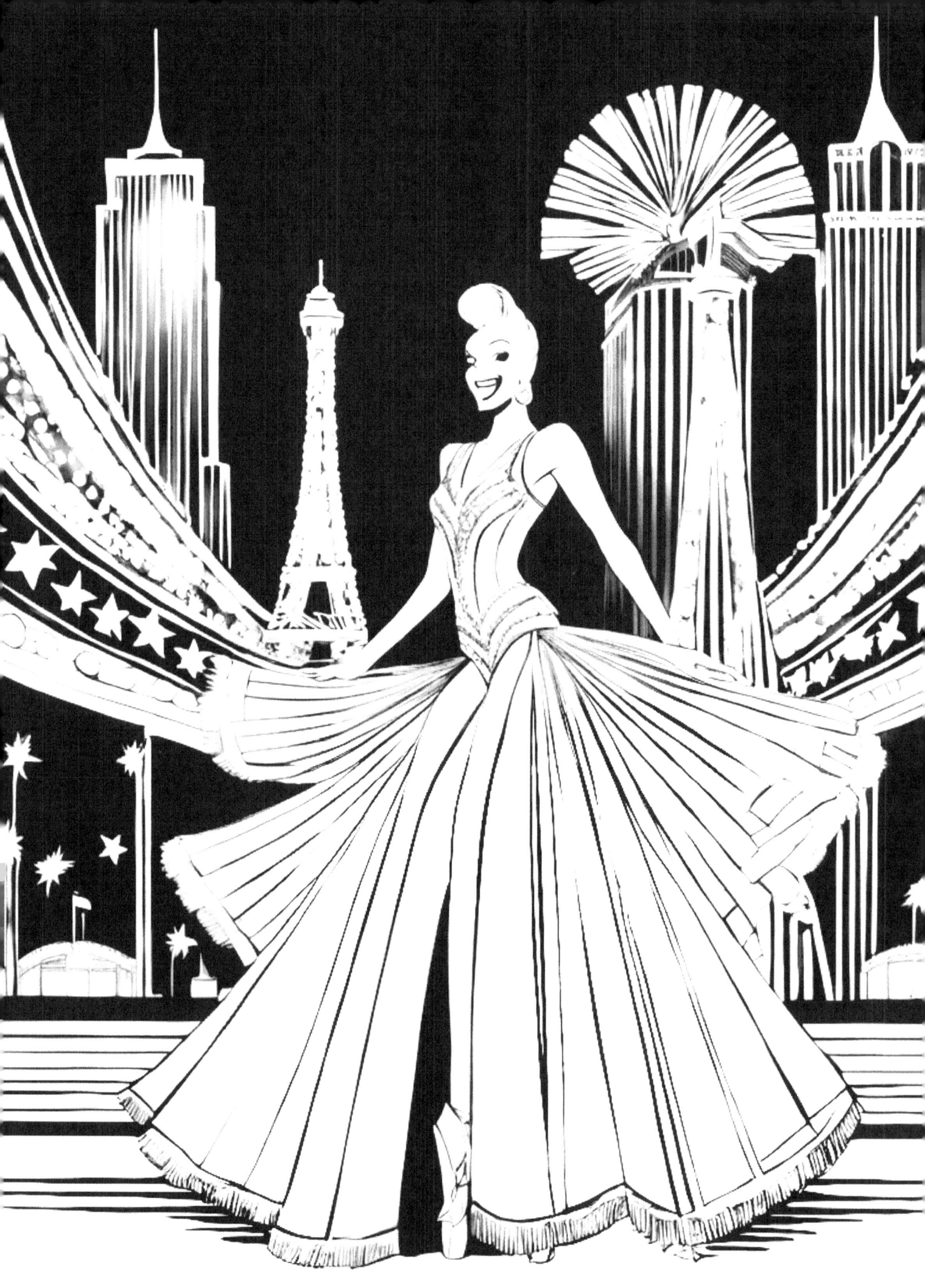

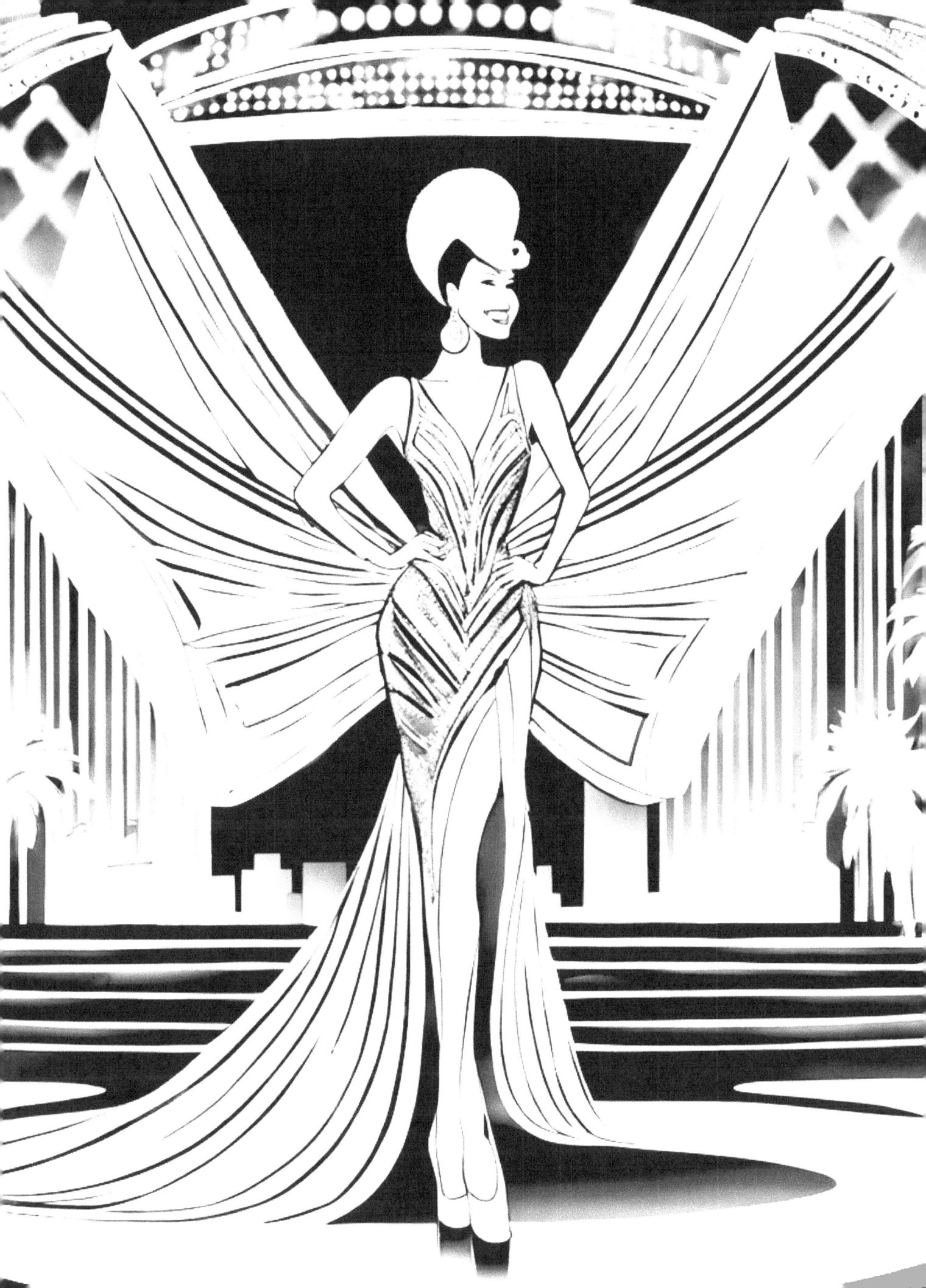